Starting and Funding Your Own Business: An Entrepreneur's Guide to Finance

Written By
Raymond Joseph Pierlioni

Table of Contents

Chapter 1: Introduction to Entrepreneurial Finance

Welcome to Starting and Funding Your Own Business: An Entrepreneur's Guide to Finance! This book is designed to help aspiring entrepreneurs like you learn about the financial side of starting and running a successful business.

In this chapter, we will explore the basics of entrepreneurial finance, including the importance of financial planning, the key financial concepts you need to know, and the various sources of funding available to entrepreneurs.

Financial planning is critical to the success of any business, including startups. It helps you identify and manage financial risks, anticipate future expenses, and allocate resources efficiently. Without a solid financial plan, you may run out of money before your business has a chance to succeed.

To create a financial plan, you need to first determine your startup costs. This includes everything from equipment and supplies to legal and accounting fees. You also need to consider your ongoing expenses, such as rent, utilities, and salaries. Once you have a clear idea of your costs, you can start looking at funding options.

There are several sources of funding available to entrepreneurs, including loans, grants, and equity financing. Loans and grants are often available through government agencies or private organizations. Equity financing involves selling shares of your business to investors in exchange for capital.

In addition to these traditional funding sources, there are also alternative options such as crowdfunding and peer-to-peer lending. Crowdfunding platforms allow you to raise money from a large number of people, often in exchange for rewards or equity. Peer-to-peer lending platforms connect borrowers with individual lenders who are willing to provide financing.

Remember, financial planning is an ongoing process. As your business grows and evolves, you will need to revise your plan to reflect changing circumstances. By taking the time to create a solid financial plan, you can increase your chances of success and build a strong foundation for your business.

Key Financial Concepts

Before you can create a financial plan, you need to understand some of the key concepts that are central to entrepreneurial finance. These include:

- Revenue: This is the total amount of money that your business earns from sales or other sources.
- Expenses: These are the costs associated with running your business, such as rent, salaries, and materials.
- Profit: This is the amount of money that your business earns after you subtract your expenses from your revenue.
- Cash flow: This is the amount of money that is coming in and going out of your business on a regular basis.
- Break-even point: This is the point at which your revenue equals your expenses, and you begin to make a profit.

- Capital: This is the amount of money that you have available to invest in your business.
- Debt: This is money that you owe to lenders or other creditors.
- Equity: This is the value of your business that is owned by shareholders.
- Assets: These are items of value that your business owns, such as equipment or property.
- Liabilities: These are debts that your business owes to others, such as loans or bills.

Sources of Funding

Once you have a basic understanding of these key financial concepts, you can begin to explore the various sources of funding that are available to entrepreneurs. Some of the most common sources of funding include:

- Personal savings: Many entrepreneurs use their own savings to fund their businesses.
- Friends and family: You may be able to raise money from friends and family members who believe in your idea.
- Small business loans: You can apply for a loan from a bank or other financial institution.
- Grants: There are many grants available to entrepreneurs from government agencies and private organizations.
- Crowdfunding: You can raise money from a large number of people through crowdfunding platforms like Kickstarter or Indiegogo.
- Venture capital: Venture capitalists are investors who provide funding to startups in exchange for a share of the company.

- Angel investors: Angel investors are typically high net worth individuals who provide funding to startups in exchange for equity in the company.
- Incubators and accelerators: These programs provide funding, mentorship, and resources to help startups grow and succeed.
- Government programs: Many governments offer funding and other resources to help entrepreneurs start and grow their businesses.
- Corporate partnerships: Some corporations offer funding or other resources to startups in exchange for a strategic partnership.
- Strategic investors: These are investors who provide funding to startups in exchange for a strategic partnership, such as access to technology or distribution channels.

Conclusion

Entrepreneurial finance can seem daunting at first, especially if you don't have a background in business or finance. But don't worry - with a little bit of knowledge and planning, you can create a successful business that not only meets your financial goals, but also helps you achieve your personal and professional aspirations.

In this chapter, we have covered the basics of financial planning, including how to develop a financial plan, how to set financial goals, and how to track your progress. We have also introduced some key financial concepts, such as revenue, expenses, profit, and cash flow. Understanding these concepts is essential for any entrepreneur who wants to make informed financial decisions.

We also talked about the various sources of funding available to entrepreneurs, including bootstrapping, crowdfunding, angel investors, venture capitalists, and loans. Each of these sources has its own advantages and disadvantages, and choosing the right one for your business depends on a variety of factors.

In the following chapters, we will dive deeper into each of these topics to help you build a strong financial foundation for your business. We will provide more detailed information on financial planning, financial concepts, and funding sources, as well as examples and case studies to help you apply these concepts to your own business. By the end of this course, you will have the knowledge and skills you need to make sound financial decisions and build a successful and sustainable business.

Chapter 2: Creating a Business Plan

Congratulations on taking the first step in starting your own business! In order to turn your idea into a successful venture, you need to create a solid business plan. A business plan is a comprehensive document that outlines your goals, strategies, and financial projections for your business.

In this chapter, we will walk you through the process of creating a business plan, step by step.

Step 1: Define Your Business

The first step in creating a business plan is to define your business. This involves asking yourself some important questions:

- What problem does your product or service solve?
- What are the unique features or benefits of your product or service?
- Who is your target customer? What are their needs and preferences?
- What is your target market size and potential for growth?
- What is the competitive landscape in your industry?
- What are the barriers to entry for new competitors?
- What is your pricing strategy?
- What are your sales channels and distribution methods?
- What is your marketing strategy?
- What is your brand identity and messaging?
- What are your core values and mission statement?
- What are your long-term goals for the business?
- What metrics will you use to measure success?

Step 2: Conduct Market Research

Market research is a crucial part of creating a business plan. It helps you understand your target market and identify potential customers. This information will help you create effective marketing strategies and make informed decisions about pricing and product development.

Some key components of market research include:

- Identifying your target market
- Conducting surveys or focus groups to gather feedback on your product or service

- Analyzing competitors and their pricing strategies
- Studying trends in your industry
- Identifying the needs and pain points of your target audience
- Evaluating the size and growth potential of your target market
- Identifying the best channels to reach your target audience
- Determining the key decision-makers and influencers in your target market
- Researching the cultural and social factors that may affect your target market
- Analyzing the strengths and weaknesses of your competitors
- Identifying opportunities for differentiation and competitive advantage
- Studying the regulatory environment and any legal limitations or requirements

Step 3: Develop a Marketing Strategy

Once you have a clear understanding of your target market, you can develop a marketing strategy. This strategy should outline how you will reach your target customers and convince them to choose your business over competitors.

Some key components of a marketing strategy include:

- Identifying your unique selling proposition (USP)
- Developing a brand identity and messaging
- Creating a social media strategy
- Planning for advertising and promotional campaigns

- Identifying your target audience's needs and preferences
- Conducting market research to understand your competition
- Analyzing the strengths and weaknesses of your competitors
- Identifying opportunities for differentiation and competitive advantage
- Creating a content strategy for your website and social media channels
- Evaluating the effectiveness of your marketing campaigns
- Developing customer personas to understand your target audience better
- Creating a referral program to encourage word-of-mouth marketing
- Building relationships with influencers in your industry
- Creating a customer loyalty program to retain customers
- Developing partnerships with complementary businesses
- Offering discounts or promotions to first-time customers
- Creating an email marketing campaign to keep customers informed and engaged

Step 4: Outline Your Business Operations

In this section of your business plan, you will outline the day-to-day operations of your business. This includes information about:

- Your business location and facilities

- Your staffing plan and team structure
- Your production or service delivery process
- Your inventory management and supply chain
- Your quality control processes
- Your customer service policies
- Your vendor and supplier relationships
- Your equipment and technology needs
- Your legal and regulatory compliance strategies
- Your risk management plan
- Your insurance policies
- Your contingency plans for unexpected events

Step 5: Create Financial Projections

The final step in creating a business plan is to develop financial projections. This includes creating a detailed budget and forecasting your revenue and expenses for the next few years.

Some key components of financial projections include:

- Creating a cash flow statement
- Projecting revenue and expenses for the next few years
- Calculating your break-even point
- Estimating your return on investment (ROI)
- Forecasting your sales and revenue growth
- Analyzing your profit margins and cost of goods sold
- Creating a balance sheet
- Identifying potential financial risks and contingencies
- Developing a financing strategy
- Describing your financial management team and their roles

- Outlining your accounting and bookkeeping procedures
- Describing your pricing strategy and how it relates to your financial projections
- Analyzing your cash flow cycle and identifying potential cash flow issues
- Describing your capital expenditures and how they will be financed
- Describing your inventory management procedures and how they will affect your financial projections
- Outlining your tax strategy and how it will affect your financial projections
- Identifying potential sources of financing and how they will affect your financial projections

Conclusion

Creating a business plan is a crucial step in starting your own business. Not only does it provide a roadmap for the future, but it also helps you define your goals, strategies, and financial projections.

In this chapter, we have covered the key components of a business plan. However, it is important to note that these components are just the beginning. In order to create a comprehensive and effective business plan, you must be willing to dive deeper into each topic.

For example, defining your business is a crucial step, but it is not enough on its own. You must also conduct market research to truly understand your target audience and competition. This research will help you develop a marketing strategy that is tailored to your business's specific needs.

Once you have a solid understanding of your business and target audience, you can begin outlining your business operations. This includes everything from daily tasks to long-term goals. By creating a detailed plan, you can ensure that you are staying on track and moving forward.

Finally, financial projections are a key component of any business plan. By creating realistic projections, you can make informed decisions and avoid financial pitfalls.

In the following chapters, we will dive deeper into each of these topics to help you create a comprehensive and effective business plan. By the end of this process, you will have a clear understanding of your business's goals and a roadmap for success.

Chapter 3: Market Research and Analysis

Market research and analysis is a critical component of creating a successful business. It provides entrepreneurs with the necessary information to make informed decisions on various aspects of their business, including product development, pricing, and marketing strategies. This information is derived from the comprehensive analysis of the market and the identification of potential customers.

One of the key benefits of conducting market research is that it helps entrepreneurs understand their target market's preferences, needs, and behaviors. This understanding enables business owners to tailor their products and services to meet the specific needs of their customers. For example, if a business owner identifies that their target market prefers eco-friendly products, they can adjust their product line to meet this demand. By meeting the needs of their target market, businesses can create a loyal customer base that is more likely to recommend their products and services to others.

Market research is also crucial in identifying potential customers. By analyzing the demographic and psychographic characteristics of the target market, businesses can identify individuals who are most likely to purchase their products or services. This information can be used to create targeted marketing campaigns that are more likely to resonate with potential customers, increasing the chances of converting them into paying customers.

Another benefit of market research is that it helps businesses stay ahead of the curve by identifying emerging trends and technologies in their industry. This information can be used to develop new products or services that meet the evolving needs of the market, giving businesses a competitive advantage. Additionally, market research can help businesses anticipate changes in the market, allowing them to adjust their strategies accordingly and stay ahead of their competitors.

In this chapter, we will walk you through the process of conducting market research and analysis, step by step.

Step 1: Define Your Research Objectives

Market research is an essential process for businesses to collect and analyze important data that can help them make informed decisions. Before embarking on this process, it is crucial to define your research objectives to ensure that the research conducted provides valuable insights and produces desired outcomes.

To define your research objectives, you must first identify the questions you want to answer. These questions can range from understanding consumer behavior and preferences to analyzing market trends and competition. Once you have determined the questions, you need to gather relevant information to answer them. This information can include data on consumer demographics, market size and growth, and product or service features.

Furthermore, setting clear research objectives can also help you achieve desired outcomes. For instance, if you want to increase sales of a product, you can conduct market research to understand consumer needs and preferences, identify areas for improvement, and develop effective marketing strategies. Alternatively, if you want to expand your business into new markets, you can conduct research to assess market opportunities, competition, and potential barriers to entry.

In short, defining research objectives is a critical first step in conducting effective market research. It helps you identify the right questions to ask, gather relevant information, and achieve desired outcomes.

Some common research objectives include:

- Understanding your target market
- Identifying customer needs and preferences
- Analyzing competitor strategies
- Studying industry trends
- Evaluating the effectiveness of marketing campaigns
- Assessing customer satisfaction and loyalty

- Identifying emerging market opportunities
- Analyzing cultural and social factors that may affect consumer behavior
- Studying the impact of technological advancements on the market
- Analyzing the regulatory environment and legal requirements
- Identifying potential barriers to entry for new competitors
- Developing customer personas to better understand target audience
- Conducting usability testing on products or services
- Identifying opportunities for product or service differentiation
- Analyzing supply chain and logistics strategies
- Studying the impact of economic trends on the market
- Assessing the impact of environmental factors on the market
- Identifying potential partnerships or collaborations
- Analyzing the strengths and weaknesses of your business

Step 2: Determine Your Research Methodology

Once you have defined your research objectives, you need to determine your research methodology. This includes identifying the population you want to study, the data collection methods you will use, and the analysis techniques that will be applied. In addition, you may also consider the ethical implications of your study and the potential limitations of your research design. It is important to carefully consider each of these components to ensure that your study is well-designed and can provide meaningful insights into your research topic.

Some common research methodologies include:

- Surveys
- Focus groups
- Interviews
- Observational research
- Secondary research (using existing data and reports)
- Case studies
- A/B testing
- Ethnographic research
- Net Promoter Score (NPS) surveys
- Customer feedback forms
- Online analytics
- Social media monitoring
- Eye-tracking studies
- Heat maps
- Usability testing
- Field experiments
- Content analysis
- Sentiment analysis
- Big data analysis
- Correlation studies
- Meta-analysis
- Cohort analysis
- Longitudinal studies

Each methodology has its own strengths and weaknesses, and the best approach will depend on your research objectives and budget.

Step 3: Develop Your Research Instrument

Once you have determined your research methodology, you need to develop your research instrument. This is the tool or questionnaire you will use to gather data and information. The research instrument should be designed to address the research questions and objectives, and should be tested to ensure it is valid and reliable. It is important to carefully consider the wording and structure of the questions to ensure they are clear and unambiguous. The research instrument should also take into account any ethical considerations, such as protecting the confidentiality and privacy of research participants. Additionally, you may want to consider using multiple methods of data collection, such as interviews or observation, to gather a more comprehensive understanding of the research topic. Finally, it is important to pilot test the research instrument with a small sample of participants to identify any potential issues or areas for improvement before conducting the full study.

Some key components of a research instrument include:

- Clear and concise questions
- Logical flow and structure
- Appropriate scales and response options
- Avoidance of bias or leading questions
- Use of appropriate language and terminology
- Inclusion of open-ended questions for qualitative data
- Consideration of target audience and their demographics
- Piloting and testing of survey with a sample group
- Integration of survey data with other research methods
- Ethical considerations in survey design and implementation
- Clear and transparent communication of survey purpose and use of data

Before using your research instrument on a larger scale, it is crucial to conduct a pilot test. Pilot testing will help you identify any issues with your instrument's effectiveness and efficiency, and allow you to make any necessary revisions before collecting data on a larger scale. Additionally, pilot testing can give you insights into how long it takes to administer the instrument, the clarity of the instructions, and the ease with which participants can complete the instrument. Overall, conducting a pilot test is an important step in ensuring the quality of your research and the validity of your results.

Step 4: Collect and Analyze Data

Once you have developed your research instrument, it's time to collect and analyze your data. First, you should identify the population or sample that you will be studying. The population refers to the entire group of individuals that you are interested in studying, while a sample is a smaller group that you will actually study. Next, you will need to decide on the data collection method that you will use. This could include administering your survey, conducting your focus groups or interviews, or conducting your observational research. Once you have collected your data, you will need to organize it and analyze it. This may involve using statistical software or other tools to identify patterns or trends in the data. Finally, you will need to draw conclusions based on your analysis and communicate your findings to others. This could involve writing a report or presenting your results at a conference.

When analyzing your data, some key considerations include:

- Identifying trends and patterns

- Identifying outliers or unusual data points
- Comparing your data to industry benchmarks
- Interpreting your data in the context of your research objectives
- Conducting regression analysis
- Using factor analysis
- Conducting cluster analysis
- Creating decision trees
- Using machine learning algorithms
- Conducting sentiment analysis
- Using text analytics
- Conducting social network analysis
- Using data visualization techniques
- Conducting conjoint analysis
- Using customer segmentation

Step 5: Draw Conclusions and Make Recommendations

The last crucial step in market research and analysis is to draw conclusions and make recommendations based on your findings. First, it is important to review your data and ensure that it accurately answers the initial questions you set out to answer. It is also helpful to identify key insights and trends that emerged from your research. These insights and trends can provide a deeper understanding of your target market and help you make informed decisions about pricing, product development, and marketing strategies. Additionally, it may be useful to conduct further research on specific aspects of your findings to gain a more detailed understanding of your customers' needs and preferences. By taking these steps, you can maximize the potential of your market research and analysis to improve your business's performance and profitability.

Some common recommendations based on market research and analysis include:

- Adjusting pricing strategies based on customer preferences and competitor pricing
- Developing new products or services based on identified customer needs
- Refining marketing strategies based on identified customer preferences and habits
- Identifying new market opportunities based on industry trends
- Analyzing customer satisfaction and loyalty to improve retention
- Conducting usability testing to improve the user experience of products or services
- Identifying and addressing potential barriers to entry for new competitors
- Studying the impact of economic and environmental factors on the market
- Developing partnerships or collaborations with other businesses
- Analyzing the strengths and weaknesses of your competitors to inform your own strategies
- Assessing the impact of technological advancements on the market and adapting accordingly
- Identifying opportunities for product or service differentiation to create a competitive advantage
- Analyzing supply chain and logistics strategies to optimize operations and reduce costs

Conclusion

Market research and analysis is a critical part of creating a successful business. It helps you understand your target market, identify potential customers, and make informed decisions about pricing, product development, and marketing strategies. In this chapter, we have covered the key steps involved in market research and analysis, including defining research objectives, determining research methodology, developing a research instrument, collecting and analyzing data, and drawing conclusions and making recommendations based on your findings. By following these steps and conducting thorough market research, you can increase your chances of success and create a business that meets the needs and preferences of your target market.

Chapter 4: Identifying Funding Sources

Starting a business can be an exciting but daunting task. One of the most crucial steps in this process is identifying funding sources. Having access to capital is essential to get your business off the ground and sustaining it through the early stages of growth.

There are several ways to approach funding for your business. One option is to seek out venture capital, which involves finding investors who are willing to provide the financial resources you need. Another approach is to secure a business loan from a bank or other lending institution. This can be a good option if you have a solid business plan and a clear understanding of your financial needs.

In addition to these traditional sources of funding, there are also alternative options available to entrepreneurs. Crowdfunding has become increasingly popular in recent years, allowing individuals to raise money from a large number of people through online platforms. Another option is to seek out grants from government organizations or non-profits that support small business development.

In this chapter, we will explore each of these funding sources in more detail, providing you with the information you need to make an informed decision about how to finance your business. By understanding the pros and cons of each option, you can choose the best funding strategy for your unique situation and increase your chances of success.

Self-Funding

Self-funding, also known as bootstrapping, is a common way for entrepreneurs to fund their business ventures. This method involves using personal savings, credit cards, or other personal assets to finance the business. Self-funding can be an attractive option for entrepreneurs as it allows them to retain control over their business and avoid the pressure of debt financing. However, it is important to note that self-funding can also be risky, as it involves investing a significant amount of personal funds into the business. This means that entrepreneurs must carefully balance the need for funding with the potential risks involved.

One of the advantages of self-funding is that it allows entrepreneurs to maintain control over their business. This means that they do not have to worry about giving up equity to outside investors or dealing with the demands of venture capitalists. With self-funding, entrepreneurs have the freedom to make decisions about their business without having to answer to anyone else.

Another benefit of self-funding is that it can help entrepreneurs avoid the pressures of debt financing. By using personal savings or other personal assets to finance their business, entrepreneurs can avoid the need to take on debt. This can help to alleviate some of the financial stress that can come with starting a new business.

However, self-funding can also be a risky proposition. Investing personal funds into a business means that entrepreneurs are putting their own financial security on the line. This can be particularly challenging for entrepreneurs who do not have a significant amount of personal savings or assets to draw from.

Despite these risks, self-funding can be a viable option for many entrepreneurs who are looking to start or grow their businesses. It is important for entrepreneurs to carefully assess their financial situation and determine if self-funding is the best option for their specific needs. This may involve creating a detailed financial plan, including projections for revenue and expenses over the short and long term.

In the end, the decision to self-fund a business or seek outside funding will depend on a variety of factors, including the entrepreneur's financial situation, the nature of the business, and the entrepreneur's goals for the future. With careful planning and a clear understanding of the risks involved, entrepreneurs can make informed decisions about how to finance their businesses and set themselves up for success.

Friends and Family

Another viable option for funding is to approach friends and family members for investment. This option is particularly useful if you have a strong personal network and can convince your loved ones to invest in your vision.

This can be a great way to get your business off the ground, especially if you are having difficulty securing funding from other sources.

When considering this option, it is important to approach the matter with caution and professionalism, as it can strain personal relationships if not handled carefully. Before approaching anyone in your personal network, it is important to have a well-developed business plan that clearly outlines the potential risks and rewards associated with the investment. Additionally, it is important to establish clear expectations and communicate openly and honestly with your potential investors about the potential risks and benefits of investing in your business.

To avoid any potential misunderstandings, it is also a good idea to have a formal investment agreement in place before any money changes hands. This agreement should outline the terms of the investment, including the amount invested, the expected return on investment, and any potential risks associated with the investment. By taking these precautions and approaching the matter with professionalism and care, you can ensure that your personal relationships remain intact while also securing the funding you need to make your business a success.

Crowdfunding

Crowdfunding is a relatively new way to raise funds for a business. This financing model has gained significant traction in recent years, as it offers entrepreneurs and businesses an alternative method for securing capital to start or grow their ventures. The concept behind crowdfunding is simple - instead of relying on a few large investors or traditional sources of funding such as banks, businesses leverage online platforms to solicit contributions from a large number of people, often referred to as backers or supporters. In exchange for their financial support, backers typically receive rewards or equity in the business, depending on the type of crowdfunding campaign.

One of the biggest advantages of crowdfunding is that it provides businesses with a unique opportunity to build a community of supporters who are invested in their vision and mission. This community can be an invaluable asset for entrepreneurs, as it not only provides them with the necessary capital to pursue their goals but also offers them access to a network of potential customers, partners, and advocates. In addition, crowdfunding can help businesses to validate their products or services, as it allows them to test the market and gather feedback from their backers.

However, while crowdfunding can be a powerful tool for raising capital and building a community of supporters, it is important to note that it is not without its challenges. One of the biggest obstacles for businesses is the increasing competition in the crowdfunding market, which makes it difficult to stand out and capture the attention of potential backers. As a result, businesses need to carefully plan and execute their crowdfunding campaigns to ensure they are effective and successful.

To maximize the potential of your crowdfunding campaign, it is crucial to develop a comprehensive strategy that aligns with your business goals and values. This strategy should include a clear and concise description of your business, highlighting its unique value proposition, and the benefits of investing in your campaign. Additionally, it is important to identify and engage with your target audience, using social media, email marketing, and other channels to raise awareness and generate interest in your campaign.

Furthermore, it is essential to create compelling content, such as videos, images, and infographics, that effectively communicates your story and resonates with your audience.

Another key element of a successful crowdfunding campaign is the rewards or equity offered to backers. These incentives should be carefully crafted to appeal to your target audience, while also providing value for your business. For example, you might offer early access to your product, exclusive discounts, or personalized experiences to your backers. Alternatively, if you are offering equity in your business, it is important to clearly communicate the potential returns and risks associated with the investment.

In summary, crowdfunding can be a powerful tool for entrepreneurs and businesses to raise capital and build a community of supporters. However, it is important to carefully plan and execute your campaign to ensure it is effective and successful. By developing a comprehensive strategy, engaging with your target audience, creating compelling content, and offering attractive incentives, you can maximize the potential of crowdfunding as a fundraising tool for your business.

Angel Investors

Angel investors are an important part of the startup ecosystem as they provide early-stage funding for businesses. These investors are typically high net worth individuals who are looking to invest in startups with high growth potential. They are often successful entrepreneurs themselves, and can bring years of experience and industry knowledge to the table.

One of the biggest benefits of working with angel investors is the access to funding that they provide. Startups often struggle to secure funding in the early stages of their development, and angel investors can help bridge that gap. This can be especially beneficial for entrepreneurs who have a great idea but lack the financial resources to get it off the ground.

In addition to providing funding, angel investors can also offer valuable insights and guidance to entrepreneurs. They can provide mentorship and support throughout the startup journey, helping entrepreneurs navigate the challenges of running a business. Moreover, they can provide valuable connections to other professionals and investors in the industry, which can be instrumental in helping startups grow and succeed.

Another benefit of working with angel investors is the flexibility that they offer. Unlike traditional lenders, angel investors are often more willing to take risks on early-stage startups. They understand that startups can be risky investments, but are willing to take that risk in exchange for the potential rewards. This can be especially helpful for entrepreneurs who are just starting out and may not have a proven track record of success.

However, it is important for entrepreneurs to carefully consider the terms of any agreement with an angel investor. While these investors can provide valuable support, they may also require a significant equity stake in the business. This can limit the entrepreneur's control over the business and can make it more difficult to secure additional funding in the future.

Overall, angel investors can be a valuable resource for startups looking to grow and succeed. They provide early-stage funding, valuable insights and guidance, and can open doors to new markets and opportunities. However, entrepreneurs must carefully consider the terms of any agreement and ensure that they are comfortable with the level of control that the investor will have over the business. With the right partnership, angel investors can be an instrumental part of a startup's success story.

Venture Capitalists

Venture capitalists (VCs) are a critical part of the startup ecosystem, providing funding to high-growth startups who have already achieved some level of success. In exchange for their investment, VCs receive a percentage of equity in the business, typically requiring a significant share of ownership to compensate for the risks they are taking on.

However, it's important to note that VCs often require a high degree of control over the business they are investing in. This can include board seats, voting rights, and other mechanisms to ensure that their interests are aligned with those of the business. Additionally, VCs may require significant changes to the business model or management team in order to maximize the potential for growth and profitability.

Despite these demands, partnering with a VC can provide significant benefits to a startup. VCs typically bring valuable industry expertise and connections, helping to open doors to new markets and opportunities. Moreover, they can provide mentorship and support to the management team, helping to navigate the challenges of scaling a business.

Another important benefit of working with a VC is access to additional funding. Once a startup has secured funding from a VC, it may be easier to secure additional rounds of funding from other investors who see the potential for growth and profitability. This can be particularly helpful for startups that are operating in a competitive market and need additional resources to stay ahead of the competition.

However, working with a VC is not without its challenges. VCs typically have high expectations for the businesses they invest in, and may require significant changes to the business model or management team in order to maximize the potential for growth and profitability. Additionally, VCs may have a short-term focus on maximizing returns, which can sometimes conflict with the long-term goals of the business.

Ultimately, the decision to partner with a VC is a complex one that requires careful consideration of the potential benefits and drawbacks. It's important for entrepreneurs to have a clear understanding of their business goals and the support they need to achieve them before making any decisions regarding funding.

In addition to VCs, there are a variety of other funding sources available to startups. These include self-funding, crowdfunding, angel investors, and small business administration (SBA) loans. Each of these options has its own advantages and disadvantages, and entrepreneurs should carefully consider their options before making any decisions regarding funding.

Self-funding, also known as bootstrapping, involves using personal savings or other personal assets to finance the business. This can be an attractive option for entrepreneurs as it allows them to retain control over their business and avoid the pressure of debt financing. However, it can also be a risky proposition, as it involves investing a significant amount of personal funds into the business.

Crowdfunding is another option for startups looking to secure funding. Crowdfunding involves leveraging online platforms to solicit contributions from a large number of people, often referred to as backers or supporters. In exchange for their financial support, backers typically receive rewards or equity in the business, depending on the type of crowdfunding campaign. Crowdfunding can be a powerful tool for raising capital and building a community of supporters, but it requires careful planning and execution to be effective.

Angel investors are another important funding source for startups. Angel investors are typically high net worth individuals who are looking to invest in startups with high growth potential. They can provide early-stage funding, valuable insights and guidance, and can open doors to new markets and opportunities. However, entrepreneurs must carefully consider the terms of any agreement and ensure that they are comfortable with the level of control that the investor will have over the business.

Finally, small business administration (SBA) loans are a good option for startups that have a strong business plan but are unable to secure funding from traditional sources such as banks. SBA loans can be more accessible than other types of funding, but they require extensive documentation and financial reporting.

In conclusion, identifying funding sources is a critical step in starting and growing a successful business. While each funding source has its own advantages and disadvantages, it's important for entrepreneurs to carefully consider their options and approach potential investors or lenders with professionalism and confidence. With the right funding, entrepreneurs can turn their vision into a successful and sustainable business.

Small Business Administration (SBA) Loans

The Small Business Administration (SBA) is an invaluable resource for entrepreneurs and small business owners looking to start or grow a business. The agency provides a wide range of programs and services designed to support small businesses, including loans, counseling, training, and technical assistance.

One of the most popular services offered by the SBA is its loan program. SBA loans can be a good option for small business owners who are unable to secure funding from traditional sources, such as banks. These loans are designed to help small businesses access the capital they need to start, expand, or operate their businesses.

SBA loans are available to businesses of all sizes and can be used for a wide range of purposes, including working capital, inventory, equipment, and real estate. The loan terms and interest rates offered by the SBA are generally more favorable than those offered by traditional lenders, making them an attractive option for small business owners who are looking to save money and get the financing they need to grow their businesses.

When applying for an SBA loan, it's important to have a strong business plan in place. This plan should outline your goals, strategies, and financial projections for the business. You should also be prepared to provide detailed financial statements, tax returns, and other documentation to support your loan application. While the process may seem daunting at first, the resources and support available through the SBA can help you navigate the process and increase your chances of success.

In addition to its loan program, the SBA also provides a range of counseling and training services to help small business owners succeed. These services include one-on-one counseling, group training sessions, and online resources. Whether you're just starting out or looking to grow your business, the SBA's counseling and training programs can provide you with the tools and knowledge you need to succeed.

Another valuable resource offered by the SBA is its technical assistance program. This program provides small businesses with access to experts in a wide range of fields, including accounting, marketing, and legal services. These experts can provide guidance and support to help small business owners overcome common challenges and grow their businesses.

Overall, the Small Business Administration plays a critical role in supporting the growth and development of small businesses across the country. Whether you're looking to start a new business or grow an existing one, the resources and services offered by the SBA can help you succeed. From loans to counseling to technical assistance, the SBA has the tools and knowledge you need to turn your entrepreneurial vision into a reality.

Conclusion

Identifying funding sources is a crucial aspect of starting and growing a successful business. This is because, without adequate funding, a business cannot survive. There are several options available for entrepreneurs to raise money, including venture capital, angel investors, crowdfunding, and traditional bank loans. Each option comes with its own set of pros and cons, and it is important to carefully evaluate them before making a decision.

In addition to considering funding options, it is also essential to create a strong business plan. Your business plan should include an executive summary, market analysis, financial projections, and a clear description of your products or services. This will help potential investors or lenders understand your business and determine whether or not they want to invest in it.

Once you have identified your funding sources and created a strong business plan, it's time to approach potential investors or lenders with professionalism and confidence. This means being prepared to answer tough questions about your business, including your revenue model, target market, and growth strategy. It also means having a clear understanding of the terms and conditions of any funding offer and being prepared to negotiate if necessary.

With the right funding and a solid business plan, you can turn your entrepreneurial vision into a successful and sustainable business that can grow and thrive for years to come.

Chapter 5: Bootstrapping Your Business

Starting a business can be an expensive endeavor, and it's not always easy to secure external funding. Fortunately, there are ways to launch and grow your business without relying on outside funding. This chapter will explore the concept of bootstrapping, or self-funding your business, and provide tips on how to make it work for you.

Start Small

Bootstrapping your business can be a challenging but rewarding experience. By starting small, you can ensure that you have a solid foundation for your business and validate your idea before investing significant resources. However, starting small doesn't mean that you should limit your ambition or settle for mediocrity. Instead, it means that you should be strategic and intentional in your approach to growth.

One way to achieve this is by focusing on generating revenue as quickly as possible. This means identifying your target market and creating a product or service that meets their needs and solves their problems. By emphasizing revenue generation, you can build a sustainable business that can eventually attract external funding if needed.

Another way to achieve growth while bootstrapping is by being resourceful and creative. This means finding innovative ways to solve problems and deliver value to your customers, even with limited resources. For example, you might leverage social media to build your brand and reach your target audience, or use open-source software to reduce your technology costs.

Moreover, bootstrapping can help you build a lean and agile business model that can adapt to changing market conditions. By focusing on efficiency and effectiveness, you can find ways to streamline your operations and deliver more value to your customers. This can help you stay ahead of the competition and create a sustainable advantage for your business.

In addition, bootstrapping can help you develop a mindset of resilience and self-reliance that can serve you well in the long run. By learning how to do more with less, you can become more resourceful and creative in your work, and develop a culture of continuous improvement and experimentation. This can help you stay nimble and adaptable in the face of uncertainty and change.

Therefore, bootstrapping can be a smart strategy for any entrepreneur who wants to build a successful business while minimizing risk and maximizing value. By starting small, focusing on revenue generation, being resourceful and creative, building a lean and agile business model, and developing a mindset of resilience and self-reliance, you can create a business that is sustainable, scalable, and successful.

Keep Overhead Low

When starting a business, it's important to keep overhead costs as low as possible. Overhead costs are expenses that are not directly tied to the production or sale of a product or service, such as rent, utilities, and office supplies. By keeping these costs low, you can maximize your profits and reinvest in your business.

One way to keep overhead low is to work from home. This eliminates the need for office space and the associated costs such as rent, utilities, and office supplies. Working from home also allows for a more flexible work schedule and can reduce commuting time and costs.

Another way to keep overhead low is to use open-source software. Open-source software is free to use and can provide many of the same features as paid software. This can save your business a significant amount of money in software licensing fees.

Buying used equipment is another way to keep overhead low. Used equipment is often much cheaper than new equipment and can still be in good condition. Consider purchasing used furniture, computers, and other equipment to save money.

Renting office space on a short-term basis or sharing office space with another business can also help reduce expenses. This can be a great option if your business is just starting out and you don't need a full-time office space.

Outsourcing certain tasks to freelancers or contractors can also help reduce costs while still getting the job done. For example, you might outsource your accounting or web design to a freelancer instead of hiring a full-time employee.

Negotiating with suppliers for better prices on materials or services is another way to keep overhead costs low. If you can get a better price on the materials you need for your product or service, you can reduce your expenses and increase your profit margins.

Finally, investing in employee training and development can help increase productivity and efficiency, leading to cost savings in the long run. By providing your employees with the skills they need to do their job more effectively, you can reduce errors and improve customer satisfaction.

In summary, there are many ways to keep overhead costs low when starting a business. Working from home, using open-source software, buying used equipment, renting office space on a short-term basis, outsourcing tasks, negotiating with suppliers, and investing in employee training and development are all effective strategies. By keeping your overhead costs low, you can maximize your profits and reinvest in your business.

Be Resourceful

Bootstrapping requires an exceptional level of resourcefulness. This means that you must proactively explore creative solutions to problems, while maximizing the resources you have available. For instance, you might consider reaching out to your personal network for advice or assistance, or bartering services with other businesses to save money.

Another way to optimize your resources is by creating a streamlined and efficient workflow. This can help you to save time and money by reducing waste and redundancies. For example, you could examine your current processes and identify areas where you could automate or outsource tasks, to help you focus on your core competencies.

Moreover, being resourceful means thinking outside the box and being open to exploring new ideas and approaches. You might consider developing non-traditional revenue streams, such as affiliate marketing, subscription services, or product bundling. Alternatively, you could explore alternative financing options, such as crowdfunding or peer-to-peer lending, to raise capital without giving up equity in your business.

Finally, being resourceful requires a willingness to take calculated risks and embrace failure as a learning opportunity. This means being open to experimentation and pivoting your strategies as needed. By being adaptable and resilient, you can overcome challenges and seize opportunities that might otherwise be missed.

In summary, being resourceful is a critical element of bootstrapping your business. By proactively seeking creative solutions to problems, optimizing your resources, thinking outside the box, and embracing risk and failure, you can build a successful and sustainable business without relying on external funding.

The Importance of Revenue Generation

When launching a new business, it is important to prioritize revenue generation above all else. A focus on sales and marketing efforts can help you generate revenue quickly, which is key to building a sustainable business. By prioritizing revenue generation, you can ensure that your business is able to generate the necessary funds to cover expenses and grow over time.

One way to emphasize revenue generation is by creating a robust sales and marketing strategy. This may involve conducting market research to identify potential customers, developing a pricing strategy that is competitive and profitable, and creating marketing materials that effectively communicate the value of your product or service.

Another important factor to consider is customer retention. While generating new revenue is important, it is equally important to retain existing customers and build long-term relationships with them. This can be accomplished through exceptional customer service, ongoing communication, and the development of loyalty programs or other incentives.

In addition, it is important to regularly track and analyze your revenue generation efforts to ensure that you are on track to meet your business goals. By measuring the success of your sales and marketing initiatives, you can identify areas for improvement and adjust your strategy accordingly.

By prioritizing revenue generation and taking a strategic approach to sales and marketing, you can build a successful and sustainable business that is well-positioned for long-term growth.

Investing in Yourself is Critical for Business Growth

As a bootstrapped business owner, investing in yourself is critical for the growth and success of your business. By continuously improving your skills and knowledge, you can stay ahead of the competition, make better decisions, and create more value for your customers.

One way to invest in yourself is by taking online courses. There are a plethora of online courses available, covering topics such as marketing, sales, leadership, and finance. These courses can help you gain new skills and knowledge that are directly applicable to your business. Additionally, online courses are often affordable and flexible, allowing you to learn at your own pace and on your own schedule.

Another way to invest in yourself is by attending industry events. Industry events provide an opportunity to learn from experts, network with peers, and gain insights into the latest trends and best practices in your industry. Attending conferences, trade shows, and workshops can also help you build relationships with potential customers and partners, and increase your visibility in the industry.

Networking with other entrepreneurs is also a valuable way to invest in yourself. By connecting with other entrepreneurs, you can learn from their experiences, gain new perspectives, and build relationships that can lead to future opportunities. Networking can also provide emotional support and encouragement, which can be especially valuable when facing the challenges of entrepreneurship.

In addition to these activities, investing in yourself can also involve reading business books and publications, listening to podcasts, and seeking out mentorship from more experienced entrepreneurs. These activities can provide new insights, help you stay motivated and inspired, and give you access to a wealth of knowledge and experience.

Ultimately, investing in yourself is critical for the growth and success of your business. By continuously improving your skills and knowledge, you can become a more effective leader, make better decisions, and create more value for your customers. Additionally, investing in yourself can help you stay motivated, inspired, and passionate about your business, even in the face of challenges and setbacks.

The Importance of Patience in Building a Business

Building a successful business is an exciting and challenging journey that requires persistence and dedication. One of the most important things to keep in mind when embarking on this journey is the importance of patience. Building a business takes time, and it's essential to have a long-term perspective and be willing to invest the effort needed to grow your business gradually and steadily.

One of the most significant benefits of taking a patient approach to building your business is that it provides you with the opportunity to build a strong foundation for long-term growth. This foundation includes things like developing a clear mission and vision for your business, building a strong team, and establishing a loyal customer base. By taking the time to focus on these critical elements, you can create a business that is rooted in a strong set of values and principles, one that can withstand the ups and downs that inevitably come with entrepreneurship.

It's important to remember that while external funding can be a powerful tool for accelerating growth, it's not always the best solution for every business. Taking on debt or giving up equity too early can put your business at risk and limit your long-term potential. Instead, by focusing on building your business gradually and organically, you can ensure that you're growing in a way that aligns with your values and goals.

Another benefit of taking a patient approach to building your business is that it allows you to learn and grow along the way. This means being open to feedback and continuously seeking out new knowledge and skills that can help you improve your business. By treating each challenge as an opportunity to learn and grow, you can develop a mindset of curiosity and resilience that will serve you well in the long run.

In conclusion, building a successful business takes time and patience. By taking a slow and steady approach, you can build a strong foundation for long-term growth, develop a culture of learning and growth, and ensure that you're growing in a way that aligns with your values and goals. While external funding can be a powerful tool for accelerating growth, it's important to remember that it's not always the best solution for every business. By focusing on the things that matter most and being patient along the way, you can build a successful and sustainable business that you can be proud of.

Conclusion

Bootstrapping your business can be a challenging but rewarding experience. By starting small, keeping overhead low, being resourceful, emphasizing revenue generation, investing in yourself, and being patient, you can build a successful business without relying on external funding. While bootstrapping is not for everyone, it can be a great way to maintain control over your business and build a sustainable foundation for long-term success.

One way to start small is by identifying a niche market that you can serve with your product or service. By focusing on a specific market, you can tailor your offerings to meet the needs of that market and differentiate yourself from competitors.

Another way to keep overhead low is by using technology to automate tasks and streamline processes. For example, you can use software to manage your finances, track inventory, and communicate with customers.

Being resourceful means finding creative solutions to problems rather than relying on traditional methods. This can involve networking with other entrepreneurs, bartering services, or finding alternative sources of funding.

Emphasizing revenue generation means focusing on activities that generate revenue rather than those that do not. For example, you might prioritize sales and marketing efforts over administrative tasks.

Investing in yourself means continually learning and improving your skills. This can involve taking courses, attending conferences, or seeking mentorship from other successful entrepreneurs.

Being patient means understanding that success takes time and being willing to put in the work to achieve your goals. It also means being flexible and willing to adapt your approach as needed.

By following these principles, you can build a successful business without relying on external funding. While bootstrapping is not without its challenges, it can be a great way to maintain control over your business and build a sustainable foundation for long-term success.

Chapter 6: Small Business Loans and Grants

Starting and growing a business requires capital, and for many entrepreneurs, this means seeking out financing options such as loans and grants. In this chapter, we'll explore the different types of small business loans and grants available, and provide guidance on how to find and apply for funding.

Small business loans can be obtained from a variety of sources, including banks, credit unions, and online lenders. Some loans require collateral, while others are unsecured. The interest rates and repayment terms can vary widely, so it's important to shop around and compare options before choosing a lender.

Grants, on the other hand, are funds that do not need to be repaid. They are typically awarded to businesses that meet certain criteria, such as being owned by a woman or a minority, or operating in a specific industry or geographic region. Grants can be obtained from government agencies, non-profit organizations, and private foundations.

In order to find and apply for small business loans and grants, it's important to do your research and understand the requirements and application process for each funding option. This may involve filling out detailed applications, providing financial statements and business plans, and meeting with lenders or grant administrators.

By exploring the different financing options available and taking the time to research and prepare your applications, you can increase your chances of obtaining the funding you need to start or grow your small business.

Types of Small Business Loans

There are many types of small business loans available, each with its own terms and requirements. Some common types of small business loans include:

- SBA Loans: These are loans guaranteed by the Small Business Administration, which can be used for a variety of purposes including working capital, equipment purchases, and real estate acquisition.
- Business Lines of Credit: These are revolving lines of credit that can be used for short-term financing needs such as inventory purchases or unexpected expenses.
- Term Loans: These are fixed-term loans that can be used for a variety of purposes including equipment purchases, working capital, and expansion.
- Invoice Financing: This is a type of financing that allows businesses to borrow money against outstanding invoices, providing cash flow while they wait for payment.

How to Qualify for a Small Business Loan

In order to obtain a small business loan, there are several pieces of information that you will need to provide to the lender. These include your business plan, financial statements, and credit history. The lender will use this information to evaluate your creditworthiness and assess whether or not you are a good candidate for financing.

It is important to note that there are several factors that may impact your ability to qualify for a loan. These factors include your credit score, revenue history, and cash flow. Additionally, the lender may consider other factors such as the industry in which your business operates and the overall economic climate.

Furthermore, it is important to have a strong understanding of your business and its financials in order to be successful in obtaining a loan. This includes being able to articulate your business's goals and objectives, as well as its strengths and weaknesses. It may also be helpful to have a detailed plan for how you intend to use the loan funds, as this can help to demonstrate your ability to manage your business finances effectively.

Overall, obtaining a small business loan can be a complex process, but with the right preparation and understanding of the lender's requirements, it is possible to secure the financing that you need to grow and expand your business.

Types of Small Business Grants

Small business grants are a form of non-repayable funding that can be used to finance business operations. Unlike loans, grants do not need to be paid back, which makes them an attractive option for many entrepreneurs. Some common types of small business grants include:

- Government Grants: These are grants provided by federal or state governments for a variety of purposes including research and development, hiring and training employees, and community development.
- Private Grants: These are grants provided by private foundations, corporations, and other organizations to support specific industries or business types.
- Crowdfunding: This is a type of financing that involves raising funds from a large group of people through online platforms such as Kickstarter or Indiegogo.

How to Find and Apply for Small Business Grants

Finding and applying for small business grants can be a time-consuming process, but it can be worth the effort for businesses that are able to secure funding. One important tip is to cast a wide net in your search for grants, as there are many different organizations and institutions offering funding opportunities. In addition to researching online databases and directories such as Grants.gov or the Foundation Center, you may also want to reach out to local business associations and community organizations for information on available grants.

When you have identified potential grants, it is important to spend time reviewing the application requirements and making sure that your business meets the eligibility criteria. This may involve gathering financial information, creating a business plan, and outlining the ways in which your business will use the grant funds.

Once you have prepared a strong application that addresses the grant's goals and requirements, be sure to submit it before the deadline and follow up as needed. Remember that even if you do not secure funding on your first attempt, there may be additional opportunities in the future, so it is important to stay informed and continue to pursue grants that are a good fit for your business.

Conclusion

Small business loans and grants can provide valuable funding for entrepreneurs looking to start or grow their businesses. However, it's not always easy to secure these funds. In order to increase your chances of success, you need to have a comprehensive understanding of the different types of financing that are available. By researching and preparing strong applications, you can make a compelling case for why your business deserves funding.

One type of financing option is a small business loan. These loans are typically offered by banks and other financial institutions. They can be secured or unsecured, and they may come with a variety of terms and conditions. Secured loans require collateral, such as property or equipment, while unsecured loans do not. The interest rates on these loans can vary widely, so it's important to shop around for the best deal.

Another option is to seek out grants. Grants are funds that are provided by government agencies, non-profit organizations, and other entities. They are typically offered to businesses that are engaged in work that benefits the community or a particular group of people. Grants may be available for a variety of purposes, including research and development, marketing, and workforce training.

It's also possible to pursue a combination of loans and grants. This approach can provide more flexibility and may help you to get the funding you need while minimizing your debt burden. However, it's important to carefully evaluate your financing options and choose the option that is best for your business.

By taking the time to understand the different types of financing that are available, and by preparing strong applications, you can increase your chances of securing the funding you need to achieve your business goals. With careful planning and execution, you can turn your business dreams into a reality.

Chapter 7: Crowdfunding Your Business

Crowdfunding has emerged as a popular alternative to traditional methods of financing for entrepreneurs looking to start or grow their businesses. This innovative funding model has disrupted the way businesses are funded by allowing entrepreneurs to pitch their ideas to a large group of investors through online platforms. In this chapter, we will delve into the intricacies of crowdfunding, including the various types of crowdfunding, the importance of creating a well-planned crowdfunding campaign, and the advantages and disadvantages of relying on crowdfunding to finance your business.

One of the key benefits of crowdfunding is that it allows entrepreneurs to tap into a wider pool of potential investors than would be possible through traditional financing methods. Moreover, crowdfunding campaigns provide an opportunity for entrepreneurs to test their ideas in the market and receive feedback from backers before bringing their products or services to market. However, it is important to note that crowdfunding is not without its drawbacks. For instance, entrepreneurs must be prepared to share a portion of their ownership or profits with their backers, and crowdfunding campaigns can be time-consuming and challenging to execute successfully.

Despite these challenges, crowdfunding has proven to be a powerful tool for entrepreneurs looking to finance their businesses. By leveraging the power of the internet and social media, entrepreneurs can reach a vast audience of potential investors and generate significant interest and support for their ideas. With the right planning and execution, crowdfunding can be a highly effective way to raise the funds needed to bring your business to life.

What is Crowdfunding?

Crowdfunding is becoming an increasingly popular way for individuals and businesses to raise money. This method involves soliciting funds from a large group of people, usually through online platforms like Kickstarter, Indiegogo, or GoFundMe. Crowdfunding can be used to raise money for many different purposes, such as launching a new product or service, financing a creative project like a movie or album, or even helping someone in need.

One of the key benefits of crowdfunding is that it allows individuals and businesses to access capital that they might not be able to obtain through traditional means. This is especially true for startups or small businesses that may not have a lot of resources or a long track record of success. By leveraging the power of the crowd, these companies can raise funds quickly and easily, often with minimal upfront costs.

Another advantage of crowdfunding is that it allows backers to feel more connected to the projects or companies they support. Rather than simply making a donation and never hearing anything more, backers often receive updates on the progress of the project, and may even have the opportunity to provide feedback or get involved in other ways. This can create a sense of community and engagement that is not always possible with other forms of fundraising.

Of course, there are also some potential risks and drawbacks to crowdfunding. For example, there is always the possibility that a campaign will not meet its funding goals, leaving the project or company without the necessary resources to move forward. Additionally, some campaigns may not be fully transparent about their goals or how they plan to use the funds they raise, which can lead to disillusionment or distrust among backers.

Despite these challenges, crowdfunding remains a powerful tool for raising funds and building communities around innovative ideas and projects. As the field continues to evolve, it will be interesting to see how crowdfunding platforms and strategies continue to adapt to meet the changing needs of entrepreneurs and investors alike.

Types of Crowdfunding

There are several types of crowdfunding, including:

- Rewards-Based Crowdfunding: This is the most common type of crowdfunding, in which backers receive a reward in exchange for their support. Rewards can range from early access to a product to a mention in the company's marketing materials.
- Equity-Based Crowdfunding: This type of crowdfunding allows backers to invest in a company in exchange for equity or a share of the profits.
- Debt-Based Crowdfunding: This is a type of crowdfunding in which backers lend money to a company in exchange for repayment with interest.

Creating a Successful Crowdfunding Campaign

Creating a successful crowdfunding campaign requires careful planning and execution. Here are some tips for creating a successful campaign:

- Set realistic goals: Be sure to set a realistic fundraising goal that reflects your actual funding needs.
- Offer attractive rewards: Offer rewards that are valuable and relevant to your backers, and that help to build buzz and excitement around your campaign.
- Tell a compelling story: Your crowdfunding campaign should tell a story that resonates with your audience and inspires them to support your business.
- Promote your campaign: Promote your campaign through social media, email, and other channels to reach a wide audience.
- Provide regular updates: Keep your backers informed about the progress of your campaign, and provide regular updates on your business and product development.

Benefits and Drawbacks of Crowdfunding

Crowdfunding can be a powerful tool for entrepreneurs, offering access to capital and the ability to test market demand for their products or services. However, there are also some drawbacks to consider, including:

- Time-consuming: Crowdfunding campaigns require significant time and effort to create and manage.
- Uncertainty: There is no guarantee that your crowdfunding campaign will be successful, and it can be difficult to predict how much funding you will be able to raise.
- Equity dilution: Equity-based crowdfunding can result in dilution of ownership for existing shareholders.

Conclusion

Crowdfunding is a great way to raise funds for your business. There are many different types of crowdfunding, such as equity crowdfunding, donation-based crowdfunding, and rewards-based crowdfunding. With equity crowdfunding, investors receive shares in your company in exchange for their investment. With donation-based crowdfunding, donors give money to support a cause or project they believe in, without expecting anything in return. Rewards-based crowdfunding involves offering perks or rewards to backers who contribute to your campaign.

To create a successful crowdfunding campaign, it's important to follow best practices. This includes setting a realistic funding goal, creating a compelling pitch video, and offering attractive perks or rewards to backers. You should also promote your campaign on social media and other channels to reach a larger audience.

Despite its benefits, crowdfunding may not be the right financing option for every business. It's important to carefully evaluate whether it aligns with your goals and values, and to consider the potential drawbacks, such as the time and effort required to run a campaign, and the potential loss of control over your business if you choose equity crowdfunding. By weighing the pros and cons and making an informed decision, you can determine whether crowdfunding is the right choice for your business.

Chapter 8: Venture Capital and Angel Investors

VWhen it comes to funding for startups and early-stage businesses, there are a variety of options available. Venture capital and angel investors, however, are two of the most notable sources of funding for these types of enterprises.

Venture capital firms typically invest in businesses that have already established some traction and are looking to scale their operations. In exchange for funding, venture capitalists often seek a significant equity stake in the business and may also require a board seat or other forms of control.

Angel investors, on the other hand, are typically high net worth individuals who invest their own money in early-stage businesses. While they may not provide as much funding as a venture capital firm, angel investors often bring valuable experience and connections to the table, which can be incredibly beneficial for a young company.

While both venture capital and angel investors can provide benefits to startups and early-stage businesses, each has its own set of drawbacks as well. For example, venture capital firms may have strict investment criteria that can be difficult for some businesses to meet. Additionally, the terms of a venture capital deal can be complex and lengthy, requiring significant legal and financial resources to negotiate.

In contrast, angel investors may not have the same level of due diligence or oversight as a venture capital firm, which can lead to potential conflicts down the line. Furthermore, angel investors may not have the same level of industry expertise or connections as a venture capitalist, which can limit the resources they are able to bring to the table.

If you are considering pursuing funding from venture capital or angel investors, it is important to begin preparing your business early on. This might involve developing a detailed business plan, establishing a strong online presence, and building relationships with potential investors.

What is Venture Capital?

When it comes to funding a startup or early-stage company, there are many different options available. However, venture capital is often seen as one of the most attractive forms of financing for companies that are looking to grow and scale quickly. Venture capital firms can provide significant funding that can help startups to invest in their business, develop new products or services, and expand their operations. In exchange for their investment, venture capital firms may receive equity in the company, which can help to align their interests with those of the startup. This can be beneficial for both parties, as it allows the venture capital firm to share in the success of the company and provides the startup with a source of funding that is aligned with their long-term goals.

One of the key benefits of venture capital financing is that it can provide startups with access to a wide range of resources and expertise. Venture capital firms typically have significant experience working with startups and can provide valuable guidance and support to help them navigate the challenges of early-stage growth. This can include everything from business strategy and operations to marketing and sales, as well as access to a wide network of industry contacts and potential customers.

Another advantage of venture capital financing is that it can provide startups with the resources they need to scale their operations quickly. This can be especially important for companies that are operating in fast-moving industries or facing significant competition. By providing funding and resources for growth, venture capital firms can help startups to stay ahead of the curve and outpace their competitors.

However, it's important to note that there are also certain drawbacks to venture capital financing that startups should be aware of. For example, venture capital firms often require significant ownership stakes in the companies they invest in, which can dilute the ownership of the founders and other stakeholders. Additionally, venture capital firms may have strict requirements and expectations for the companies they invest in, which can be challenging for startups to meet.

Overall, venture capital financing can be a powerful tool for startups and early-stage companies that are looking to grow and scale quickly. By providing access to funding, resources, and expertise, venture capital firms can help startups to achieve their goals and build successful businesses. However, it's important for startups to carefully consider the benefits and drawbacks of venture capital financing and to explore all of their financing options before making a decision about which path to pursue.

What are Angel Investors?

Angel investors are a crucial source of funding for startups and early-stage businesses. These investors are typically high net worth individuals who are looking for opportunities to invest their money in innovative and promising ventures. In exchange for their investment, angel investors typically receive equity in the company, which can help them earn a return on their investment if the company is successful.

In addition to providing financial support, angel investors often bring a wealth of experience and expertise to the table. Many angel investors are successful entrepreneurs themselves, and they can provide valuable advice and guidance to the companies they invest in. They may also have extensive networks of contacts that can help the company grow and succeed.

Overall, angel investors play a vital role in the startup ecosystem, providing much-needed funding and support to innovative and promising ventures. Without the support of these investors, many startups would struggle to get off the ground, and the world would miss out on the many innovative products and services they could have created.

Differences between Venture Capital and Angel Investors

The main differences between venture capital and angel investors are:

- Investment Size: Venture capital firms typically invest larger sums of money than angel investors.
- Timing: Venture capital firms generally invest in more established companies, while angel investors are more likely to invest in very early-stage startups.
- Control: Venture capital firms often require a seat on the board of directors and may exert more control over the company than angel investors.

Benefits and Drawbacks of Venture Capital and Angel Investors

Venture capital and angel investors can provide significant benefits to startups and early-stage businesses, including access to capital, expertise, and industry connections. However, there are also drawbacks to consider, such as:

- Equity Dilution: Both venture capital and angel investors typically require equity in the company in exchange for their investment, which can dilute the ownership of existing shareholders.
- Control: Venture capital firms may exert more control over the company than the founders are comfortable with.
- High Expectations: Both venture capital firms and angel investors have high expectations for return on investment, and may pressure the company to prioritize growth over profitability.

Preparing Your Business for Investment

Before seeking investment from venture capital firms or angel investors, it's important to ensure that your business is ready. Here are some steps you can take to prepare your business for investment:

- Develop a solid business plan that clearly outlines your vision, goals, and strategies for growth.
- Build a strong team with experience and expertise in your industry.
- Develop a strong product or service that solves a real problem in the market.
- Create a clear path to profitability and a strategy for scaling your business.
- Establish relationships with potential investors and industry experts.

Conclusion

Venture capital and angel investors can provide valuable funding and resources to startups and early-stage businesses. While venture capital firms are typically larger and invest later in a company's life cycle, angel investors are usually individuals who provide funding earlier on. Additionally, angel investors often invest smaller amounts of money but can provide valuable mentorship and connections.

To prepare your business for investment, it is important to focus on developing a strong business plan that clearly outlines your company's goals and strategies for growth. In addition, building a strong team with a diverse set of skills and experiences can increase your chances of success and attract investors who are looking for a solid management team.

Establishing relationships with potential investors and industry experts is also critical. Attend networking events and conferences to meet potential investors and learn from industry leaders. Consider joining an accelerator program or incubator to gain access to resources and mentorship.

Overall, while both venture capital and angel investors can provide critical funding, it's important to weigh the benefits and drawbacks of each option and determine which is best for your business's specific needs and goals.

Chapter 9: Financial Statements and Projections

Financial statements and projections are crucial elements for entrepreneurs who are seeking funding or managing their businesses. They are also valuable tools for analyzing financial performance and making strategic decisions. In this chapter, we will delve into the significance of financial statements and projections, their role in managing a business, and how they can be used for forecasting future trends. We will also examine the various types of financial statements, such as balance sheets, income statements, and cash flow statements, and discuss the key elements of each. Additionally, we will provide guidance on how to prepare financial projections for your business, including forecasting revenue, expenses, and cash flow. Finally, we will touch on the importance of financial modeling and how it can be used to test and refine your financial projections. By the end of this chapter, you will have a comprehensive understanding of the role financial statements and projections play in the success of a business and how to create accurate and useful financial projections for your own business needs.

The Importance of Financial Statements and Projections

Financial statements and projections are important for several reasons:

- They provide insights into the financial health of your business, including its revenue, expenses, and profitability.
- They help you track your progress towards your financial goals and make informed decisions about the future of your business.
- They provide critical information for potential investors and lenders, who will want to see evidence of your business's financial performance before committing to funding.

Types of Financial Statements

There are three main types of financial statements:

- Income Statement: This statement shows your business's revenue, expenses, and net income or loss over a specified period of time. It provides a snapshot of your business's profitability.
- Balance Sheet: This statement shows your business's assets, liabilities, and equity at a specific point in time. It provides a snapshot of your business's financial position.
- Cash Flow Statement: This statement shows your business's inflows and outflows of cash over a specified period of time. It provides insights into your business's liquidity and cash management.

Preparing Financial Projections

Financial projections are estimates of your business's future financial performance based on assumptions about revenue, expenses, and other financial variables. To prepare financial projections for your business, follow these steps:

- Identify your revenue streams: Estimate your revenue based on your pricing strategy, market size, and growth projections.
- Estimate your expenses: Estimate your expenses based on your operational costs, marketing expenses, and other costs associated with running your business.
- Determine your break-even point: Calculate the amount of revenue you need to generate to cover your expenses and break even.
- Create a cash flow forecast: Based on your revenue and expense estimates, create a cash flow forecast that shows your inflows and outflows of cash over time.
- Use financial modeling tools: There are many tools available to help you create financial projections, such as spreadsheets and accounting software.

Interpreting Financial Statements and Projections

Interpreting financial statements and projections requires an understanding of key financial ratios and metrics. Here are a few important ones to keep in mind:

- Gross Profit Margin: This measures the profitability of your products or services after accounting for the cost of goods sold.
- Net Profit Margin: This measures your business's overall profitability after accounting for all expenses.
- Debt-to-Equity Ratio: This measures the amount of debt your business has relative to equity.
- Return on Investment (ROI): This measures the return you're getting on your investment in your business.

Conclusion

Financial statements and projections are crucial for entrepreneurs seeking funding and managing their businesses. With accurate and well-supported financial statements and projections, you can provide important information to potential investors and lenders, track your progress towards your financial goals, and make informed decisions about the future of your business. However, it is not enough to simply prepare financial statements and projections; you must also understand the key ratios and metrics that underlie them. By analyzing these ratios and metrics, you can gain deeper insights into your business's financial health and make strategic decisions to improve its performance.

For example, one key ratio to consider is the debt-to-equity ratio, which measures the amount of debt your business has relative to its equity. A high debt-to-equity ratio can indicate that your business is heavily reliant on debt financing, which can be risky in the long term. On the other hand, a low debt-to-equity ratio may suggest that your business is not taking advantage of opportunities to invest in its growth. By understanding this ratio and others like it, you can make more informed decisions about how to structure your financing and investments.

In addition to financial ratios, you should also consider other metrics that can help you track your business's performance over time. For example, you may want to monitor your cash flow, which measures the amount of cash coming in and going out of your business. By analyzing your cash flow over time, you can identify trends and potential issues that may affect your business's financial health.

Overall, financial statements and projections are essential tools for entrepreneurs, but they are only as useful as the insights you can draw from them. By understanding key ratios and metrics and using them to inform your decision-making, you can take your business to the next level and achieve your financial goals.

Chapter 10: Accounting for Your Business

Starting and running a business comes with many challenges, and one of the most critical aspects of managing a business is accounting. Accounting is the process of recording, classifying, and summarizing financial transactions to produce financial statements that provide insight into your business's financial performance. The financial statements, such as the income statement, balance sheet, and cash flow statement, are crucial for decision-making and financial planning.

In this chapter, we will delve into the importance of accounting and how it can help you manage your business more effectively. We will explore the different types of financial statements and explain how to prepare them accurately. Additionally, we will discuss various bookkeeping methods and accounting software that can help make the accounting process more efficient.

By understanding accounting principles and applying them to your business, you can gain a better understanding of your business's financial health, make informed decisions, and plan for future growth. Whether you're a new business owner or a seasoned entrepreneur, this chapter will provide you with valuable insights to help you manage your finances effectively.

Types of Financial Statements

Financial statements are reports that provide information about your business's financial performance. The three main types of financial statements are:

- Income Statement: This statement shows your business's revenue, expenses, and net income or loss over a specified period of time.
- Balance Sheet: This statement shows your business's assets, liabilities, and equity at a specific point in time.
- Cash Flow Statement: This statement shows your business's inflows and outflows of cash over a specified period of time.

Bookkeeping Methods

Bookkeeping is the process of recording financial transactions. There are two main bookkeeping methods:

- Cash Basis Accounting: This method records transactions when cash is received or paid.
- Accrual Basis Accounting: This method records transactions when they occur, regardless of when cash is received or paid.

Accrual basis accounting is the preferred method for most businesses because it provides a more accurate picture of your business's financial performance. By recognizing revenues when they are earned and expenses when they are incurred, accrual basis accounting ensures that your financial statements reflect the true financial position of your business. This is especially important for businesses with complex operations, as cash basis accounting may not provide an accurate representation of their financial performance. Additionally, accrual basis accounting allows for better tracking of accounts payable and accounts receivable, making it easier to manage your cash flow and plan for future expenses. By providing a more comprehensive view of your business's financial performance, accrual basis accounting can help you make more informed decisions and improve your overall profitability in the long run.

Accounting Software

Accounting software can make the accounting process easier and more efficient for businesses of all sizes. It offers a variety of features and benefits that can help automate many of the time-consuming tasks associated with accounting. For example, accounting software can help businesses create and send invoices, track expenses, manage payroll, and generate financial reports. These capabilities not only save time but also help ensure accuracy and consistency in financial reporting.

When choosing accounting software, there are several factors to consider. One of the most important considerations is cost. Some accounting software options are expensive and may not be cost-effective for smaller businesses. On the other hand, some free options may not offer the same level of functionality and support as paid options. It is important to carefully evaluate the cost of each option in relation to its features and capabilities to determine which is the best fit for your business.

Another important consideration is ease of use. The accounting software should be user-friendly and easy to navigate, with clear instructions and support available if needed. This is particularly important for businesses that do not have dedicated accounting staff and may need to rely on other team members to manage the software.

Integration with other systems is also an important consideration. Many accounting software options offer integration with other business systems, such as customer relationship management (CRM) software, inventory management systems, and e-commerce platforms. This can help streamline business operations and ensure that all systems are working together seamlessly.

In addition to these key factors, businesses should also consider the specific accounting needs of their organization. For example, businesses that deal with large amounts of inventory may need accounting software with robust inventory management capabilities. Similarly, businesses that operate in multiple countries may need accounting software that can handle multiple currencies and tax regulations.

Some popular accounting software options include QuickBooks, Xero, and Wave. QuickBooks is a well-known and widely used option that offers a range of features for businesses of all sizes. Xero is another popular option that offers cloud-based accounting software with a strong focus on automation and integration with other systems. Wave is a free option that offers basic accounting features and is particularly well-suited to smaller businesses.

Overall, accounting software is a powerful tool for businesses that can greatly improve the efficiency and accuracy of financial reporting. By carefully evaluating the key factors and choosing the right software for your business, you can ensure that your accounting processes are as effective and efficient as possible.

Managing Accounts Receivable and Accounts Payable

Accounts receivable are amounts owed to your business by customers, while accounts payable are amounts your business owes to vendors or suppliers. Managing accounts receivable and accounts payable is essential for maintaining positive cash flow. To manage accounts receivable and accounts payable, follow these tips:

- Invoice promptly: Send invoices as soon as possible to ensure timely payment.
- Follow up on late payments: Send reminders or make phone calls to customers who are past due on payments.

- Negotiate payment terms: Negotiate favorable payment terms with vendors or suppliers to help manage your cash flow.
- Monitor your cash flow regularly to avoid surprises.
- Consider implementing a cash reserve or emergency fund to handle unexpected expenses.
- Review your expenses regularly to identify areas where you can cut costs.
- Consider offering discounts for early payments to incentivize customers to pay on time.

Hiring an Accountant

If you're not comfortable managing your business's accounting on your own, consider hiring an accountant. An accountant can provide valuable advice on financial management and help ensure that your financial statements are accurate and compliant with accounting standards.

When it comes to managing your business's finances, it's important to understand the many different factors that can impact your bottom line. From taxes and regulatory compliance to cash flow and budgeting, there are countless considerations that come into play.

One of the most important decisions you'll make as a business owner is whether to handle your accounting in-house or outsource it to a professional. While some small business owners may be able to handle their own accounting, many others find it overwhelming or simply don't have the time or expertise to manage it effectively.

If you're in the latter category, it's important to consider hiring an accountant to help you navigate the many complexities of financial management. An experienced accountant can provide valuable guidance on everything from budgeting and forecasting to tax planning and regulatory compliance.

In addition to helping you manage your finances, an accountant can also play an important role in helping you grow your business. By providing strategic advice on funding, expansion, and other key issues, an accountant can help you make informed decisions that lead to long-term success.

So if you're struggling to keep up with your business's finances or simply need some expert guidance, don't hesitate to reach out to a qualified accountant. With their help, you can take control of your finances and build a thriving business for years to come.

Conclusion

Accounting is a fundamental aspect of managing your business. By understanding the basics of financial statements, bookkeeping methods, and accounting software, you can better manage your business's finances and make informed decisions. For example, having a clear understanding of your cash flow, expenses, and revenues is essential to making informed decisions that can help you grow your business. By keeping accurate financial statements and using reliable bookkeeping methods, you can gain a better understanding of your business's financial health and identify areas for improvement.

Another crucial aspect of managing your business's finances is managing accounts receivable and accounts payable. This involves tracking what your business owes to others and what is owed to your business. By staying on top of these accounts, you can ensure positive cash flow and avoid late payments or penalties.

If you're not comfortable managing your business's accounting on your own, consider hiring an accountant to provide valuable advice and ensure compliance with accounting standards. An accountant can help you understand complex financial data and provide insights into areas where you can save money or reduce costs. They can also help you stay compliant with tax regulations and avoid costly penalties. With the help of an experienced accountant, you can focus on growing your business while leaving the financial details to the experts.

Chapter 11: Managing Cash Flow

Managing cash flow is a crucial component of running a successful business. It allows you to track the movement of money in and out of your company, which is essential for ensuring that you have enough funds to cover expenses, pay bills, and make necessary investments. By maintaining a healthy cash flow, you can also position your business for future growth.

One of the most important aspects of managing cash flow is understanding the importance of cash flow management. This involves the careful monitoring and control of your cash inflows and outflows to ensure that your business has enough cash on hand to cover its obligations and make strategic investments. Effective cash flow management involves developing a comprehensive understanding of your business's financial health, including its revenue streams, expenses, and debt.

In addition to understanding the importance of cash flow management, it's also essential to understand the components of a cash flow statement. A cash flow statement is a financial statement that shows the movement of cash in and out of your business over a specified period of time. It includes three primary components: operating cash flow, investing cash flow, and financing cash flow.

Operating cash flow refers to the cash that your business generates from its primary operations, such as sales and expenses. Investing cash flow refers to the cash that your business uses to invest in assets, such as property, equipment, or other businesses. Financing cash flow refers to the cash that your business uses to finance its operations, such as borrowing or repaying loans, issuing or buying back stock, or paying dividends.

Understanding these components of a cash flow statement can provide valuable insights into how your business is generating and using its cash. It can also help you identify potential areas for improvement and make informed decisions about future investments and expenses.

Strategies for improving cash flow can include negotiating payment terms with suppliers, creating a budget, and reducing expenses. For example, negotiating payment terms with suppliers can help you maintain positive cash flow by ensuring that you have enough time to pay your bills without incurring late fees or penalties. Creating a budget can help you identify potential areas where you can reduce expenses, such as unnecessary office supplies or equipment.

Another important strategy for improving cash flow is to forecast your cash flow. Cash flow forecasting involves predicting your business's future cash inflows and outflows to better manage your cash flow. By accurately forecasting your cash flow, you can identify potential cash shortfalls and take proactive steps to address them before they become a problem.

In conclusion, managing cash flow is a critical aspect of running a successful business. By understanding the importance of cash flow management, the components of a cash flow statement, and strategies for improving your cash flow, you can position your business for long-term success. By maintaining a healthy cash flow, you can ensure that your business has the necessary funds to cover its obligations, make strategic investments, and grow over time.

The Importance of Cash Flow Management

Cash flow management is one of the most critical aspects of ensuring that your business remains financially stable and experiences growth. The movement of cash in and out of your business is a crucial element of effective cash flow management. By monitoring this movement, you will be able to identify areas of your business that need improvement and take advantage of growth opportunities. By ensuring that you have enough cash on hand to meet your obligations, you can achieve financial stability for your business. It is essential to have an effective cash management system in place to ensure that your business can cover expenses and make investments that can drive growth. In summary, effective cash management is critical to the success of your business, and it involves monitoring and managing the movement of cash in and out of your business to ensure that you have enough cash on hand to meet your obligations and take advantage of growth opportunities.

Components of a Cash Flow Statement

A cash flow statement is a financial statement that shows the movement of cash in and out of your business over a specified period of time. The three components of a cash flow statement are:

- Operating Activities: This section shows cash flows related to your business's primary operations, such as sales and expenses.
- Investing Activities: This section shows cash flows related to investments in assets such as property, equipment, or other businesses.
- Financing Activities: This section shows cash flows related to financing activities, such as borrowing or repaying loans, issuing or buying back stock, or paying dividends.

Strategies for Improving Cash Flow

Improving your cash flow involves managing your business's cash inflows and outflows. Here are some strategies to consider:

- Increase sales: Increasing sales can help increase cash inflows and improve cash flow.
- Reduce expenses: Reducing expenses can help decrease cash outflows and improve cash flow.

- Manage accounts receivable and accounts payable: Managing accounts receivable and accounts payable is important for maintaining positive cash flow. Invoice promptly and follow up on late payments to improve accounts receivable management. Negotiate favorable payment terms with vendors or suppliers to help manage accounts payable.
- Control inventory: Managing inventory levels can help prevent excess inventory and free up cash for other uses.
- Use cash flow forecasting: Cash flow forecasting involves predicting your business's future cash inflows and outflows to better manage your cash flow.

Conclusion

Effective cash flow management is a crucial aspect of ensuring the financial stability and growth of your business. Cash flow management involves monitoring and managing the movement of cash in and out of your business to ensure that you have enough cash on hand to meet your financial obligations and take advantage of growth opportunities.

One of the key tools for effective cash flow management is a cash flow statement. A cash flow statement provides a detailed breakdown of the movement of cash in and out of your business over a specified period of time. By keeping an up-to-date cash flow statement, you can have a clear picture of your business's financial situation and identify potential areas for improvement.

There are several strategies that you can use to improve your cash flow. One approach is to increase sales by implementing marketing and sales strategies that are designed to attract new customers and retain existing ones. Another way to improve cash flow is to reduce expenses by cutting unnecessary costs and negotiating better deals with vendors.

Managing accounts receivable and accounts payable is also an important part of cash flow management. By collecting payments from customers more quickly and delaying payments to vendors when possible, you can improve your cash position. You may also want to consider offering incentives for early payment to help improve your cash flow.

Controlling inventory is another key aspect of cash flow management. By managing your inventory levels more effectively, you can reduce the amount of cash tied up in inventory and free up resources for other uses. This may involve implementing inventory management software or other tools to help you track inventory levels and anticipate future demand.

Finally, using cash flow forecasting can help you anticipate potential cash flow issues and take proactive steps to address them. By forecasting your cash flow needs and identifying potential shortfalls, you can take steps to ensure that you always have enough cash on hand to meet your obligations and pursue new opportunities.

In addition to these strategies, it is also important to regularly review and update your cash flow management plan. As your business grows and evolves, your cash flow needs may change, so it is important to regularly reassess your strategies and make adjustments as needed.

By implementing these strategies and effectively managing your cash flow, you can improve the financial health of your business and position it for long-term success. With a solid cash flow management plan in place, you can ensure that your business has the necessary resources to meet its financial obligations and achieve its growth goals.

Chapter 12: Tax Planning for Small Businesses

As a small business owner, effective tax planning can be a crucial component in managing your finances, minimizing your tax liability, and improving your business's financial health. By taking a strategic approach to tax planning, you can identify opportunities to increase cash flow, reduce tax expenses, and optimize your tax position. In this chapter, we will cover the basics of tax planning for small businesses, including types of taxes, planning strategies, and common deductions. Additionally, we will provide detailed examples and scenarios to help you better understand the concepts and apply them to your own business. Whether you are just starting out or looking to refine your existing tax planning strategy, this chapter will help you make informed decisions about your business's financial future. So buckle up and get ready to take your tax planning to the next level!

Types of Taxes

There are several types of taxes that small businesses may be subject to, including:

- Income tax: Income tax is a tax on the profits earned by your business.
- Self-employment tax: Self-employment tax is a tax on your business's net earnings, which includes both your personal income and your business's profits.
- Payroll tax: Payroll tax is a tax on the wages you pay to your employees.
- Sales tax: Sales tax is a tax on the sale of goods or services in certain states.

Tax Planning Strategies

Tax planning involves taking steps to minimize your tax liability while remaining compliant with the tax laws. Here are some tax planning strategies to consider:

- Keep accurate records: Accurate record-keeping is essential for minimizing your tax liability and avoiding penalties for noncompliance.
- Take advantage of deductions: Deductions are expenses that can be subtracted from your business's taxable income, reducing your overall tax liability. Common deductions include office expenses, travel expenses, and advertising expenses.
- Consider entity selection: The type of business entity you choose can affect your tax liability. For example, a sole proprietorship may be subject to self-employment tax, while a corporation may be subject to double taxation.
- Plan for estimated taxes: Estimated taxes are quarterly payments made to the IRS to cover your tax liability for the year. Planning for estimated

taxes can help you avoid penalties and interest for underpayment.

- Work with a tax professional: A tax professional can help you navigate the complex tax laws and identify opportunities for tax savings.

Common Tax Deductions

Here are some common tax deductions that small businesses may be eligible for:

- Home office deduction: If you work from home, you may be able to deduct a portion of your home expenses, such as rent or mortgage interest, utilities, and insurance.
- Vehicle expenses: If you use your vehicle for business purposes, you may be able to deduct the expenses related to its use, such as gas, maintenance, and insurance.
- Employee expenses: You can deduct the expenses related to hiring and paying employees, including salaries, wages, and benefits.
- Equipment and supplies: You can deduct the expenses related to purchasing and maintaining equipment and supplies, such as computers, software, and office furniture.

Conclusion

Effective tax planning is crucial to the financial health of your small business. A solid tax plan can help you minimize your tax liability, increase your cash flow, and ensure long-term success. In order to achieve this, there are several key steps that you should take.

First, it is important to keep accurate records of all financial transactions. This will not only help you identify potential tax savings, but it will also ensure that you are in compliance with the tax laws.

Second, taking advantage of deductions is an essential part of tax planning. By understanding which expenses are deductible, you can reduce your taxable income and lower your tax liability.

Third, considering entity selection is crucial when it comes to tax planning. Choosing the right business structure can have a significant impact on your tax liability.

Fourth, planning for estimated taxes is an important step in effective tax planning. By estimating your tax liability and making estimated tax payments throughout the year, you can avoid penalties and interest charges.

Lastly, working with a tax professional can help you identify opportunities for tax savings and ensure that you are in compliance with the tax laws. With the help of a tax professional, you can develop a comprehensive tax plan that is tailored to the specific needs of your small business.

By following these key steps and staying up-to-date on the latest tax laws and regulations, you can position your small business for long-term success and financial stability.

Chapter 13: Exit Strategies and Selling Your Business

As a small business owner, it is important to think about the future of your business, and planning for an exit strategy should be a part of that. This can include considering whether you plan to sell your business or pass it down to family members. Understanding the different exit strategies available and the process of selling a business is essential.

When it comes to selling your business, there are several factors to consider, such as finding the right buyer, valuating your business, and negotiating the terms of the sale. It is important to start planning early and seek the advice of professionals who can help guide you through the process.

In addition to selling your business, there are other exit strategies available, such as merging with another company or taking your business public. Each strategy has its own advantages and disadvantages, and it is important to evaluate which strategy aligns best with your goals and objectives.

Ultimately, having a well-thought-out exit strategy can provide peace of mind and security for both you and your business. It allows you to plan for the future, minimize risks, and maximize the value of your business.

Types of Exit Strategies

There are several types of exit strategies that small business owners may consider:

- Selling the business: Selling your business involves finding a buyer who is willing to purchase your company for a fair price. This can be a lengthy process that involves valuing your business, identifying potential buyers, and negotiating a sale.

- Passing the business to family members: If you have family members who are interested in taking over the business, you may consider passing it down to them. This can involve creating a succession plan and ensuring that your family members have the skills and knowledge to run the business.
- IPO: If your business is large enough and has significant growth potential, you may consider taking your company public through an initial public offering (IPO). This involves selling shares of your company to the public in exchange for capital.
- Liquidation: Liquidation involves selling off the assets of the business and using the proceeds to pay off any debts or obligations. This is typically a last resort option when other exit strategies are not feasible.

Preparing for the Sale

Preparing for the sale of your business can take months or even years. Here are some steps you can take to prepare:

- Get your financials in order: Make sure that your financial statements are accurate and up-to-date. This can help potential buyers understand the financial health of your business.
- Identify potential buyers: Consider who might be interested in buying your business, such as competitors or investors.
- Value your business: Determine the fair market value of your business by taking into account factors such as revenue, profits, and industry trends.

- Clean up your operations: Make sure that your business is running smoothly and that your operations are streamlined.
- Seek professional advice: Consider hiring a business broker or attorney to help you with the sale process.

Selling Your Business

Selling your business involves several steps, including:

- Negotiating the sale: Once you have identified a potential buyer, you will need to negotiate the terms of the sale. This may include the purchase price, payment terms, and any contingencies.
- Due diligence: The buyer will likely conduct due diligence, which involves reviewing your financial statements, legal documents, and other business records.
- Closing the deal: Once the buyer has completed due diligence and is satisfied with the terms of the sale, you can close the deal and transfer ownership of the business.

Tax Implications

When selling your business, tax planning is a critical aspect that should not be overlooked. The tax implications of selling a business can be significant and can impact both the buyer and the seller. In order to ensure that you are able to minimize the tax consequences of selling your business, it is important to work with a tax professional who can provide guidance on the tax implications of the sale.

One of the most important aspects of tax planning for a business sale is understanding the various types of taxes that may apply. Capital gains tax, for example, is one of the most significant taxes that may be applicable to a business sale. This tax is levied on the difference between the net proceeds of the sale and the cost basis of the assets being sold. In addition to capital gains tax, corporate tax may also be applicable to the sale. This tax is levied on the profits earned by the business, and may be due even after the sale of the business.

In order to minimize the tax consequences of selling your business, it is important to work with a tax professional to develop a tax planning strategy. This may involve considering the tax-efficient structuring of the sale, such as the use of a tax-deferred exchange or an installment sale. A tax-deferred exchange allows you to defer paying taxes on the gain from the sale by reinvesting the proceeds in a similar business or property. An installment sale, on the other hand, allows you to spread the tax liability over a number of years.

Another tax planning strategy to consider is timing the sale. By carefully timing the sale, you may be able to minimize the amount of taxes owed. For example, if you are able to sell the business in a year when your overall income is lower, you may be able to reduce the amount of taxes owed on the sale.

Finally, it may be possible to reinvest the proceeds of the sale in tax-advantaged investments. This can help you minimize the amount of taxes owed on the sale, while also generating income and potential capital gains in the future.

In conclusion, tax planning is a critical aspect of selling your business. By working with a tax professional and developing a tax planning strategy, you can minimize the tax implications of the sale and make the most of your business sale. With careful planning and a clear understanding of the tax implications of the sale, you can ensure that you are able to make the most of your business sale while minimizing the tax consequences.

Conclusion

Having an exit strategy is an essential aspect of planning for the future of your business. It is crucial to keep in mind that not all exit strategies are created equal, and what may work for one business may not be suitable for another.

One common exit strategy is selling the business. This strategy can be complex, and it's essential to understand the process involved. Before selling, it's essential to prepare the business for sale. This process includes evaluating the company's financials, assets, and liabilities. Once the business is prepped, you can then start to look for potential buyers. It's essential to negotiate the terms of the sale carefully. This includes determining the selling price, payment terms, and any contingencies.

Another exit strategy is passing the business down to family members. This strategy is more common in family-owned businesses. If you plan to pass the business down to your family, it's important to have a succession plan in place. This plan should outline who will take over the business and how the transfer of ownership will occur.

No matter which exit strategy you choose, understanding the tax implications is critical. Taxes can significantly impact the sale of a business or transfer of ownership.

Consult with a tax professional to understand the tax consequences of your chosen exit strategy.

By taking the time to plan for the future, you can ensure that your business is well-positioned for success. It's important to take into account the unique characteristics of your business and choose an exit strategy that aligns with your goals and values.

Chapter 14: Legal Considerations for Entrepreneurs

Starting and running a business involves a lot of risks and challenges, and it is crucial for entrepreneurs to be aware of the legal implications of their business decisions. One of the most important legal considerations for entrepreneurs is business entity formation. Choosing the right business entity is crucial for protecting personal assets, minimizing taxes, and achieving business goals. There are several options to choose from, including sole proprietorship, partnership, limited liability company (LLC), and corporation. Each type of business entity has its own legal requirements and regulations that entrepreneurs should be familiar with.

Another key legal consideration for entrepreneurs is protecting their company's trademarks and intellectual property. Intellectual property protection is essential to maintaining the company's brand and preventing others from using their ideas or inventions without permission. Some common types of intellectual property include trademarks, patents, and copyrights. Filing for trademarks and patents can be a complicated process, so it is important to consult with an attorney or intellectual property specialist to ensure that the company's intellectual property is protected.

Employment laws are another important legal consideration for entrepreneurs. As an employer, it is important to understand the laws and regulations that govern employees. Some common employment laws include the Fair Labor Standards Act, Family and Medical Leave Act, Americans with Disabilities Act, and Title VII of the Civil Rights Act. Ensuring compliance with employment laws can help entrepreneurs avoid legal issues and maintain a positive work environment for their employees.

Contract law is also an essential aspect of doing business, and entrepreneurs must be well-versed in it. A contract is a legally binding agreement between two or more parties, and it can cover a wide range of topics, including sales agreements, employment contracts, non-disclosure agreements, and lease agreements. It is important to have contracts reviewed by an attorney to ensure that they are legally binding and protect the company's interests.

Finally, entrepreneurs are responsible for complying with various tax laws and regulations, such as income tax, payroll tax, and sales tax. Failure to comply with tax laws can result in fines, penalties, and legal action. It is important to work with a tax professional to understand the company's tax obligations and develop a tax planning strategy.

In conclusion, entrepreneurs must be well-versed in the legal considerations that come with starting and running a business. Understanding business entity formation, protecting intellectual property, complying with employment laws, understanding contract law, and complying with tax regulations are all important legal considerations for entrepreneurs. By working with legal and tax professionals, entrepreneurs can ensure that they are complying with the law, protecting their interests, and avoiding legal issues.

Business Entity Formation

One of the first legal considerations for entrepreneurs is choosing a business entity. There are several options to choose from, including:

- Sole proprietorship: A business owned and operated by one individual.
- Partnership: A business owned and operated by two or more individuals.
- Limited Liability Company (LLC): A business entity that provides the limited liability protection of a corporation with the tax benefits of a partnership.
- Corporation: A business entity that is separate from its owners and provides limited liability protection.

Choosing the right business entity is important for protecting personal assets, minimizing taxes, and achieving business goals.

Trademarks and Intellectual Property

Protecting your company's trademarks and intellectual property is crucial to maintaining your brand and preventing others from using your ideas or inventions without permission. Some common types of intellectual property include:

- Trademarks: A symbol, word, or phrase that identifies a product or service.
- Patents: Exclusive rights to an invention for a certain period of time.
- Copyrights: Exclusive rights to a creative work, such as a book, song, or software.

Filing for trademarks and patents can be a complicated process, so it is important to consult with an attorney or intellectual property specialist.

Employment Laws

As an employer, it is important to understand the laws and regulations that govern your employees. Some common employment laws include:

- Fair Labor Standards Act: Sets standards for minimum wage, overtime, and child labor.
- Family and Medical Leave Act: Requires employers to provide job-protected leave for certain family and medical reasons.
- Americans with Disabilities Act: Prohibits discrimination against individuals with disabilities in employment.
- Title VII of the Civil Rights Act: Prohibits discrimination on the basis of race, color, religion, sex, or national origin.

Violating employment laws can result in fines, penalties, and legal action, so it is important to stay up-to-date on the latest regulations.

Contracts

Contracts are an essential part of doing business, and entrepreneurs need to be familiar with contract law. A contract is a legally binding agreement between two or more parties, and it can cover a wide range of topics, including:

- Sales agreements
- Employment contracts
- Non-disclosure agreements
- Lease agreements

It is important to have contracts reviewed by an attorney to ensure that they are legally binding and protect your interests.

Taxes

Entrepreneurs must navigate various tax laws and regulations, such as income tax, payroll tax, and sales tax, in order to operate legally. Complying with these laws can be overwhelming, especially for those who are new to the business world. Failure to comply with tax laws can result in fines, penalties, and legal action, which can have a significant impact on a business's financial stability. Therefore, it is important for entrepreneurs to work with a tax professional to understand their tax obligations and develop a tax planning strategy.

Working with a tax professional is beneficial for entrepreneurs because they have the expertise to help businesses understand and comply with tax laws. A tax professional can help entrepreneurs navigate complex tax laws and regulations, optimize their tax position, and identify potential opportunities for tax savings. They can also help businesses develop a tax planning strategy that is tailored to their specific needs and goals. By working with a tax professional, entrepreneurs can avoid costly mistakes and ensure that they are in compliance with tax laws.

Income tax is one of the most important taxes that entrepreneurs need to understand. Income tax is a tax on the profits earned by a business, and it is calculated based on the taxable income of the business. The amount of income tax that a business owes depends on various factors, such as the type of business entity, the business's location, and the amount of taxable income. A tax professional can help entrepreneurs understand how income tax works and identify deductions that can reduce their overall tax liability.

Payroll tax is another tax that entrepreneurs need to understand. Payroll tax is a tax on the wages paid to employees, and it includes both the employer and employee portions of Social Security and Medicare taxes. Payroll tax can be complicated and time-consuming to calculate, especially for businesses with multiple employees. A tax professional can help entrepreneurs understand their payroll tax obligations, calculate the correct amount of tax owed, and ensure that they are in compliance with payroll tax laws.

Sales tax is another important tax that entrepreneurs need to be aware of. Sales tax is a tax on the sale of goods and services in certain states, and it is typically collected by the seller and remitted to the state. Sales tax laws can be complex, and they vary from state to state. A tax professional can help entrepreneurs understand their sales tax obligations, register for a sales tax permit, and ensure that they are collecting and remitting sales tax correctly.

In conclusion, entrepreneurs are responsible for complying with various tax laws and regulations, including income tax, payroll tax, and sales tax. Compliance with these laws is crucial for businesses to operate legally and avoid costly penalties and fines. Working with a tax professional can help entrepreneurs understand their tax obligations, optimize their tax position, and ensure compliance with tax laws. By developing a tax planning strategy and seeking professional guidance, entrepreneurs can position their businesses for long-term success and financial stability.

Conclusion

Understanding the legal considerations that come with starting and running a business is an essential component of a successful business strategy. Not only does it protect your company from legal problems, but it also ensures that your business is properly structured and managed. There are several crucial factors to consider when it comes to legal considerations, including choosing the right business entity, protecting your intellectual property, complying with employment laws, understanding contract law, and complying with tax regulations.

Choosing the right business entity is a critical decision that will impact your business's legal structure, taxation, and liability. It is essential to choose the appropriate entity for your business, whether it be a sole proprietorship, partnership, limited liability company (LLC), or corporation. Protecting your intellectual property is also crucial to safeguarding your business's unique identity and competitive edge. This may include obtaining patents, trademarks, or copyrights.

Complying with employment laws is essential for any business with employees. These laws govern various aspects of the employer-employee relationship, including hiring practices, compensation, benefits, and termination. Understanding contract law is also crucial to ensure that your business is protected when entering into agreements with vendors, suppliers, or customers. Finally, complying with tax regulations is essential to avoid penalties and ensure that your business is properly structured for tax purposes.

By working with legal and tax professionals, entrepreneurs can ensure that they are complying with the law and protecting their interests. These professionals can provide invaluable guidance and advice on the various legal considerations that come with starting and running a business. They can also help entrepreneurs navigate the complex legal landscape and avoid legal problems that could harm their business. By taking the time to understand and address these legal considerations, entrepreneurs can set their businesses up for long-term success.

Chapter 15: Case Studies of Successful Entrepreneurs

Starting and running a business is no easy feat, and it requires a lot of hard work, dedication, and perseverance. As entrepreneurs, we are constantly on the lookout for ways to improve our businesses and take them to the next level. Studying the success stories of other entrepreneurs is definitely an excellent way to learn valuable lessons and gain inspiration for our own business ventures.

In this chapter, we will explore some case studies of successful entrepreneurs and the lessons we can learn from their experiences. By doing so, we can begin to see patterns in their success stories and apply them to our own lives. We can also gain a deeper understanding of the challenges and obstacles that they faced, and how they overcame them. Additionally, by studying a variety of different success stories, we can gain insights into different industries and business models, and how they can be applied to our own ventures.

One of the key benefits of studying successful entrepreneurs is that we can learn from both their successes and their failures. By doing so, we can avoid common pitfalls and increase our chances of success. For example, we can learn from Elon Musk's willingness to think big and invest heavily in his vision, while also taking note of the production delays and rocket explosions that his companies have faced. We can also learn from Sara Blakely's persistence and dedication to her vision, despite facing numerous rejections from manufacturers.

Another benefit of studying successful entrepreneurs is that we can gain inspiration and motivation for our own businesses. By learning about the successes and achievements of others, we can see what is possible and set higher goals for ourselves. For example, learning about Oprah Winfrey's media empire can inspire us to think bigger and aim higher in our own ventures.

In addition to gaining inspiration and avoiding common pitfalls, studying successful entrepreneurs can also help us gain a deeper understanding of the business world. By learning about different industries and business models, we can broaden our knowledge and develop a more well-rounded perspective. This can be especially helpful for entrepreneurs who are just starting out and are still exploring different industries and business models.

In conclusion, studying successful entrepreneurs is an excellent way to learn valuable lessons and gain inspiration for our own business ventures. By doing so, we can avoid common pitfalls, gain insights into different industries and business models, and set higher goals for ourselves. So, let's dive into these case studies and see what we can learn from these successful entrepreneurs.

Jeff Bezos, Amazon

Jeff Bezos founded Amazon in 1994 with the goal of creating the world's most customer-centric company. He started by selling books online, but quickly expanded to other products, including music, movies, and electronics. Bezos' vision was to create a platform where customers could find anything they wanted to buy, all in one place, and have it delivered to their doorstep quickly and reliably. His focus on customer satisfaction and convenience soon made Amazon a household name and transformed the way people shop online.

Bezos' success can be attributed to his relentless pursuit of innovation and his willingness to take risks. He is known for his famous quote, "If you can't tolerate failure, you can't innovate." Bezos has never been afraid to experiment with new products and services, even if they are risky or unproven. This philosophy has allowed Amazon to continue to grow and expand into new markets, including cloud computing, streaming media, and even physical grocery stores.

One of the keys to Amazon's success has been its ability to use data to drive innovation and make informed business decisions. Bezos has always been a proponent of data-driven decision making, and Amazon has invested heavily in technology and analytics to gather and analyze customer data. This has allowed Amazon to personalize the shopping experience for each customer, recommend products they are likely to purchase, and improve the efficiency of its operations.

In addition to his focus on innovation and data, Bezos is also known for his long-term perspective and willingness to invest in the future. He famously reinvests most of Amazon's profits back into the company, rather than paying dividends to shareholders. This has allowed Amazon to make significant investments in new products and services, as well as infrastructure and logistics, which have helped the company maintain its competitive edge.

Today, Amazon is the largest online retailer in the world, with over 200 million unique visitors per month. The company has expanded to offer a wide range of products and services, including Amazon Web Services (AWS), Amazon Prime, and Amazon Alexa. Amazon's influence extends beyond just online retail, as the company has disrupted many other industries as well. Bezos' vision and leadership have played a crucial role in Amazon's success, and his legacy will continue to shape the company for years to come.

Lesson: Focus on customer satisfaction and be willing to take risks in order to innovate.

Sara Blakely, Spanx

The story of Sara Blakely and her creation of the Spanx brand is a testament to the power of perseverance and dedication. Blakely's journey from a struggling entrepreneur to a successful businesswoman is an inspiration to many.

Blakely's story began in 2000 when she was unable to find a comfortable and flattering undergarment to wear under her clothes. Frustrated with the lack of options available in the market, she decided to create her own solution. She spent two years researching and developing a prototype for a product that would address the shortcomings of traditional undergarments. Her vision was to create a product that would be comfortable, flattering, and versatile enough to wear with any outfit.

Blakely's journey was not an easy one. She faced numerous rejections from manufacturers who did not share her vision. However, she remained focused on her goal and continued to push forward. She eventually found a manufacturer who shared her vision and was willing to produce her product.

Despite finding a manufacturer, Blakely's challenges did not end there. She had to invest heavily in advertising to get her product out to the masses. She even personally went to department stores to demonstrate the product to customers. This was a risky move, but her persistence and dedication paid off in the end. Customers were impressed with the product and sales began to soar.

Today, the Spanx brand is a household name. Blakely's persistence and dedication to her vision has paid off in spades. The brand has expanded beyond undergarments and now includes a variety of clothing items. The Spanx brand has become synonymous with confidence and comfort, all thanks to the hard work and dedication of Sara Blakely.

Blakely's journey is a reminder that success does not come easy. It requires hard work, dedication, and perseverance. Her story is an inspiration to anyone who has a vision and a dream. It shows that with the right mindset and attitude, anything is possible. By setting goals, staying focused, and persevering through challenges, anyone can achieve their dreams just like Sara Blakely did with the Spanx brand.

Lesson: Don't be discouraged by rejection, and invest in advertising to promote your product.

Elon Musk, Tesla and SpaceX

Elon Musk is an innovative entrepreneur who has revolutionized the automotive and space exploration industries with his companies Tesla and SpaceX. Musk's success can be attributed to his ability to think big, his innovative ideas and his willingness to invest heavily in his vision.

Musk founded Tesla in 2003 with the goal of accelerating the world's transition to sustainable energy. The company's mission is to produce electric cars that are not only environmentally friendly but also offer superior performance and innovative features. Tesla's cars have become popular worldwide, and the company has become a leader in the production and sale of electric vehicles. The Tesla Model S, Model X and Model 3 have all received critical acclaim and have won numerous awards for their design, performance and safety features.

SpaceX, founded in 2002, is another company founded by Musk, with the goal of reducing space transportation costs and enabling the colonization of Mars. SpaceX has achieved numerous milestones in the field of space exploration, including launching the first privately-funded spacecraft to the International Space Station, and launching the Falcon Heavy, the most powerful rocket in operation today. Musk has famously stated that his ultimate goal for SpaceX is to enable humans to become a multi-planetary species.

Musk's companies have faced numerous challenges along the way, including production delays and rocket explosions, but he remains committed to his vision of advancing sustainable energy and exploring space. Musk's unwavering dedication to his goals has also led to the development of other innovative projects such as The Boring Company, which aims to revolutionize transportation by building underground tunnels for high-speed travel and Loop, an electric transportation system using underground tunnels.

Musk's success can also be attributed to his leadership style. He is known for being hands-on and involved in every aspect of his companies. He is not afraid to take risks, and he encourages his employees to do the same. He leads by example and inspires his team to think creatively and push boundaries.

In addition to his work with Tesla and SpaceX, Musk has also been involved in other ventures such as SolarCity, a company that provides solar energy systems for homes and businesses. Musk's vision for the future of energy is one that is sustainable, efficient and accessible to everyone.

Overall, Elon Musk's success can be attributed to his ability to think big, his innovative ideas, his willingness to take risks and his unwavering dedication to his vision. His companies have revolutionized the automotive and space exploration industries, and his work has inspired many people around the world. Musk's legacy will continue to influence the world for years to come.

Lesson: Think big, invest heavily in your vision, and remain committed to your goals.

Brian Chesky, Airbnb

Brian Chesky's journey in co-founding Airbnb is an inspiration to many aspiring entrepreneurs. Chesky's background in industrial design allowed him to bring a unique perspective to the company's development, emphasizing the importance of user experience and visual design.

However, Chesky and his team initially faced numerous challenges in launching Airbnb. They had to overcome regulatory hurdles in many cities, and they also had to convince people to trust strangers with their homes. To combat these issues, Chesky and his team focused on creating a safe and personalized experience for users. They implemented a system of user reviews and ratings, which helped to build trust among users and ensure that guests had a positive experience in their temporary accommodation.

As Airbnb began to gain traction and expand into new markets, Chesky continued to prioritize the company's mission of creating a unique and personalized travel experience. He recognized that travelers were looking for more than just a place to stay - they wanted to experience the local culture and connect with people from different backgrounds. To address this need, Airbnb began to offer experiences and activities led by local hosts, such as cooking classes, neighborhood tours, and language lessons.

Thanks to these innovative strategies, Airbnb has been able to disrupt the traditional hotel industry and become a leading player in the travel industry. Today, the company offers a wide range of accommodation options to suit different needs and budgets, including entire homes, apartments, and unique properties like treehouses and houseboats. Airbnb has also expanded its offerings to include experiences, activities, and even transportation options like city tours and bike rentals.

Chesky's leadership and vision have been instrumental in Airbnb's success. He has emphasized the importance of creating a positive user experience and building trust among users, which has helped to differentiate Airbnb from its competitors. Chesky has also recognized the importance of staying true to the company's mission and values, even as it has grown rapidly and faced new challenges.

In addition to his work with Airbnb, Chesky has also been involved in philanthropic efforts, including the creation of the Airbnb Community Fund, which supports local community organizations in cities around the world. Chesky has also been recognized for his leadership and innovation, receiving numerous awards and accolades for his work with Airbnb.

In conclusion, Brian Chesky's journey in co-founding Airbnb is a testament to the power of innovation, perseverance, and a dedication to creating a positive user experience. Chesky has shown that by prioritizing the needs of users and staying true to a company's mission and values, it is possible to disrupt traditional industries and achieve great success as an entrepreneur.

Lesson: Focus on creating a unique and personalized experience for your customers, and be prepared to overcome regulatory hurdles.

Oprah Winfrey, OWN Network

Oprah Winfrey is a true inspiration to entrepreneurs everywhere. Her story is a testament to the power of hard work, dedication, and perseverance. From humble beginnings, Winfrey rose to become one of the most successful and influential women in the world, with an empire that spans across various forms of media.

Winfrey's journey to success was not an easy one. She faced numerous challenges along the way, including poverty, abuse, and discrimination. However, she refused to let these obstacles define her or hold her back. Instead, she used them as motivation to work harder and achieve her goals.

One of the keys to Winfrey's success is her unwavering commitment to her vision. When she founded the OWN Network, she had a clear idea of what she wanted the network to be and the impact she wanted it to have on the world. She was determined to create a platform that would inspire and empower individuals to improve their lives and achieve their dreams. Winfrey's dedication to her vision was evident in the programming that she developed for the network. The shows were carefully curated to reflect her values and beliefs, and they spoke to the core of what she stood for.

Another key to Winfrey's success is her willingness to take risks. When she founded the OWN Network, she was entering into a highly competitive and constantly evolving industry. The cable television landscape was already crowded with established players, and launching a new network was a risky move. However, Winfrey was undeterred. She believed in her vision and was willing to take a chance on it. Her willingness to take calculated risks has been a hallmark of her career, and it has paid off many times over.

Winfrey's success is also due in part to her ability to surround herself with talented and dedicated individuals. She has a keen eye for talent and has worked with some of the best and brightest individuals in the industry. By building a strong team around her, Winfrey was able to create a network that was not only successful but also sustainable.

Today, the OWN Network is a major player in the cable television industry, and it has had a significant impact on the world of media and entertainment. It continues to inspire and empower individuals to improve their lives and achieve their dreams. Winfrey's legacy is one that will continue to influence and inspire entrepreneurs for generations to come.

In conclusion, Oprah Winfrey is a true inspiration to entrepreneurs everywhere. Her story is a testament to the power of hard work, dedication, and perseverance. By staying true to her vision, taking calculated risks, and surrounding herself with talented individuals, Winfrey was able to build an empire that has had a profound impact on the world. Her success is a reminder that anything is possible if you are willing to work hard and never give up on your dreams.

Lesson: Remain committed to your vision, invest in quality programming, and don't be afraid to take risks.

Conclusion

Studying the success stories of other entrepreneurs is an excellent way to gain inspiration, motivation, and learn valuable lessons for your own business ventures. Success stories are not just anecdotes, they are often rich sources of information about the strategies, tactics, and mindsets that successful entrepreneurs use to achieve their goals. They can provide you with insights into the challenges and obstacles that entrepreneurs face and how they overcame them. By studying these stories, you can begin to see patterns in their success and apply them to your own business.

One of the most important lessons that you can learn from successful entrepreneurs is the importance of customer satisfaction. By focusing on delivering exceptional customer experiences, you can build a loyal customer base that will return again and again to your business. This can help you grow your customer base and increase your revenue.

Another key lesson from success stories is the importance of taking risks. Entrepreneurs who take calculated risks are often the ones who are able to identify new opportunities and stay ahead of the competition. By taking risks, you can try new things and experiment with different strategies that can help you grow your business.

Persistence is also a common theme among successful entrepreneurs. The road to success is often long and winding, and there will be setbacks and failures along the way. However, by persisting through rejection and persevering through challenges, you can build a resilient mindset and stay motivated to achieve your goals.

Thinking big is another important mindset that successful entrepreneurs often have. By having a clear vision for your business and setting ambitious goals, you can motivate yourself and your team to work harder and smarter. This can help you achieve your goals faster and create a more successful business.

Creating unique experiences for your customers is also an important tactic that successful entrepreneurs use to differentiate themselves from the competition. By providing personalized experiences that cater to your customers' needs and preferences, you can build a strong brand identity and stand out in a crowded market.

Investing in quality programming and technology is also crucial to entrepreneurship success. By using the latest technology and tools, you can streamline your operations, reduce costs, and improve the overall customer experience. This can help you grow your business faster and more efficiently.

Finally, remaining committed to your vision and values is essential to building a successful business. By staying true to your mission and values, you can build a business that is authentic and sustainable. This can help you build a loyal customer base and attract top talent to your team.

In conclusion, studying the success stories of other entrepreneurs is an invaluable tool for anyone looking to start or grow a business. By learning from the experiences of others and applying their strategies and tactics to your own business, you can increase your chances of achieving success. So, take the time to study the success stories of other entrepreneurs and learn from their experiences.

www.ingramcontent.com/pod-product-compliance
Lightning Source LLC
Chambersburg PA
CBHW071137220526
45467CB00015B/1354